THE RAILWAY YEARS

The Further Reminiscences of a Truck Driver

Laurie Driver

authorHOUSE®

AuthorHouse™
1663 Liberty Drive
Bloomington, IN 47403
www.authorhouse.com
Phone: 1-800-839-8640

First published by AuthorHouse   3/8/2010

ISBN: 978-1-4490-9040-1 (sc)

Printed in the United States of America
Bloomington, Indiana

This book is printed on acid-free paper.

INTRODUCTION

The railway years, as a written work, is an elaboration and an expansion and hopefully a betterment. It is a more detailed account of a précis of written tales of life on the railways as a trailer boy and road vehicle driver. Anecdotes pertaining to The Railway years first appeared in 'This Truckin' Life,' as a somewhat truncated and expurgated version of events.

As a small part of a bigger book I could only include so much, but I think the time as come to write a full and unexpurgated version of the humorous and sometimes serious events that took place between the years of 1962 and 1976 when I was employed by British Railway's and its sister companies including NCL, Freightliner, Railfreight, etc; plus subsequent returns to the company it became, via BRS Taskforce and EXEL Logistics. BRS and Pickford's transport became a part of the railways with the nationalisation of all inland transport during the Second World War and remained so even after private hauliers started to ply their trade again after the cessation of hostilities.

The earlier part of the book is based mainly in and around Manchester and a lot of the place names and street names are within the Greater Manchester area. The later chapters take place on a national basis.

This is a series of anecdotes both humorous and serious with, I hope, the main interest being on the humour. All incidents written about in this work are true. Characters names have been changed where deemed necessary.

I have tried, as in 'This Truckin' Life', to intersperse the humorous anecdotes with informative chapters and anecdotes.

There is some repetition from the earlier book in order to keep a certain continuity and fluidity, although I have endeavoured to couch these repetitions in different terms to avoid a feeling of déjà vu. When repeated I have given the anecdotes a different slant. A number of anecdotes from the first book I have left out altogether or just alluded to so as to avoid repetition. Conversely there are a lot of hitherto untold tales that I hope will keep the reader entertained and amused.

My life on the railways started when I joined what was then the L.M. Region, at Deansgate Parcels Depot, Manchester in 1962 aged 16 coming on 17. This was not what I had planned. I was destined for finer things, or so I thought. Even so the railway years turned out to be unforgettable good times. I left the railways at age 21 in 1967 and returned two years later and stayed in various posts until 1976. This book is about the time between those years and subsequent revisits.

I returned to the railways again in the 1990's on train crew duties for a short period. This episode is also included in the following narrative. Also included is a short period that I spent working for EXEL Logistics which is the company that NCL and Rail Freight parcels became and which still employed a lot of ex railwaymen.

Front cover photograph courtesy of Alan Earnshaw.

CHAPTER 1
PRIOR TO WORKING
ON THE RAILWAY

Life on the railway. You wouldn't believe it!

It was with deception and duplicity that I was prevailed upon to start work on the railway at the Deansgate Parcels Depot in Manchester. It was in the post of a trailer boy on a local delivery round that I was to be employed. The pressure to embark on this career with the erstwhile London Midland Region of British Rail was brought to bear by a lacklustre, uninterested civil servant. My choice of career and that that I had worked in, until I was made redundant, prior to joining the L.M. Region was in the printing trade.

In 1962 I was a somewhat naïve, ingenuous and gullible youth who had led a sheltered upbringing, protected from the absurdities of life by my over protective parents. This over protective attitude now strikes me as absurd in itself. They had encouraged me to study for my U.L.C.I's, (Union of Lancashire & Cheshire Institutes) and then GCE 'O' levels with the hope that I would go on to take 'A' levels and then on to university to gain a degree. A few of my friends and classmates actually achieved those lofty heights but that, I am afraid, was not my lot.

My father, who was a plumber by trade, had told me over and again about the importance of a good education and the relevance of good exam results. 'You need a trade.' He would tell me. 'Better still if you got a degree. You don't want to be a labourer all your life, do you? You want to be better than the every day common working man,' he would say. The problem, as far as I was concerned, was that he laboured the subject to the point of distraction and I was completely fed up of hearing it. Besides, I didn't need any specific qualifications to secure an apprenticeship.

I did, though, understand my father's point of view because what he had achieved in his life he had done of his own volition. He was a Londoner, from the Lambeth area, born out of wedlock, the result of an affair his mother had conducted with a French speaking, Swiss waiter named Auguste Burnier. That affair was carried out while her husband was away at war. As a child he and his elder sister, Lou were unloved, unwanted, uncared for and maltreated. When my father was ten years of age both he and his sister were given over to the care of one of Doctor Barnardo's charitable homes where destitute children were looked after and taught a trade. For all the good Dr Barnardo's did at the time, a hard and strict regime was in force and bullying often took place. My father was put out to service at the age of fifteen and when he was old enough he joined the RAF. It was during WWII whilst in the RAF that he met and married my mother. He was an intelligent and well read person and very much a self educated man. I should have listened to him.

DR BARNARDO'S

John Thomas Barnardo was born in Dublin in 1845 and arrived in London in 1866. He found the city struggling to cope with the effects of the industrial revolution. There was a dramatic increase in the population and much of that increase was concentrated in the East End where there were rat infested slums and where poverty, disease and unemployment were rife.

It was not long after Thomas Barnardo arrived in London that an outbreak of cholera swept through the East End killing more than three thousand people and decimating the community and leaving children homeless. Thousands of youngsters were forced to sleep on the streets and take to begging.

Thomas Barnardo, shocked by what he had seen, set up a ragged school in 1867, where poor children could get a basic education and he became devoted to helping destitute children. In 1870, Barnardo opened his first home for boys in Stepney Causeway. On a regular basis he went out at night into the slum areas to find destitute boys that needed his help. His first home for boys bore the sign 'No Destitute Child Ever Refused Admission.'

The well to do Victorians of the day saw poverty as shameful and a result of laziness or vice. Thomas Barnardo, however, accepted all children and stressed that every child deserved the best start in life, whatever their background; that philosophy still inspires the charity today.

Barnardo later opened The Girl's Village Home at Barkingside, Essex; a collection of cottages situated around a green, which housed fifteen hundred girls. It was said that by the time a child left Barnardo's they were able to make their own way in the world.

The boy's Garden City, at Woodford Bridge, Essex was opened by Dr Barnardo in 1909 and it was to this home that my father was later sent whilst his sister was sent to the Girl's Village Home.

THE PRINTING TRADE &
GOLD BLOCKING

Some friends of mine had left school at fifteen years of age without any qualifications at all and were earning, what seemed to me, vast amounts of cash doing jobs that did not require any particular skill or knowledge. They seemed to be happy and possessed of a certain independence that I envied and so I rebelled, I truanted from school, my studies were abandoned and I became disruptive. Things that were totally out of character became the norm for me; I was the rebel without a cause. My father, in an attempt to stop the downward spiral of self destruction, offered to give me enough pocket money to equal my working friends' spending power on the condition that I carried on with my education, but enough was enough and I had had enough and so I left school, or as the American's would have it, I dropped out, with just a handful of qualifications to help me get the job I wanted and enable me to start earning a living wage.

It was after a few weeks into my chosen trade that my mistake was realised and just how right my father had been, came to be understood. I had abandoned one situation whereby I had to do exactly as I was told to take up another situation whereby I had to do exactly as I was told. The independence, for which I had yearned, was non existent and I didn't even earn enough to pay for a midday meal each day. I was a fool of the highest magnitude, a nincompoop that thought he knew better than his wiser and more knowledgeable elders.

That one other appointment, the chosen career, that I had undertaken before entering the world of British Rail, was as an apprentice in the printing industry. I became a Printer's Devil, in the trade of gold blocking and embossing. A printer's Devil was the name given to an apprentice or an odd job man in the printing trade. Gold blocking was not, as the name suggests, the making of blocks or ingots of the precious, yellow metal, but a specialised sector of the printing trade. It entailed printing, under pressure and heat, in gold leaf and other metallic and coloured foils.

The word blocking has two roots and comes from the fact that earlier printers cut their designs into blocks of wood and later printers etched them into blocks of brass known as dies. It was also derived from the work of a 15th century German printer named Johannes Gensfleisch Gutenberg (1397-1468), who invented movable type (c.1436), that could be set as blocks of print which improved over the years until stereotyping was developed in 1804 and whole pages could be cast. The first printed Latin Bible (1452-1455) known as the Gutenberg Bible is attributed to him. Prior to Gutenberg and before William Caxton who was the first known commercial English printer, (1422-1491), and before the invention of the wooden printing press, any and all types of simple printing was done from etched wooden blocks, usually of boxwood.

Gold blocking, as well as movable type, used dies, usually of brass, with the customer's motif, logo or name etched into them. The trade was highly skilled and precise but in the nine months that was my term of employment in that pursuit I had learned practically nothing, nix, nought, zero, zilch. I felt a little used as my duties seemed to entail nothing more than cleaning up, brewing up, running errands and operating as the general gopher and dog's body. My lot was the 'fetch me, bring me, and carry me' operative and those were chores in which I had already fulfilled an apprenticeship at home. I was more the odd-job man than the apprentice.

It was after the nine months that the owner of this enterprise, Mr Gordon Hedley, came to the conclusion that there was not the work to sustain his entire workforce. So that was it, being the last to start work at Hedley's it was fitting that I became first to go, deemed surplus to requirements, no longer needed and thus cast away on the scrapheap of unemployment. The other young Devil that was employed by Hedley, a lad a year senior to me and named Bob, who had actually started to learn the trade after my appointment, took an immediate retrograde step and was demoted back to brew boy, errand boy, dog's body and odd-job man.

J. T. Hedley's is still trading and is to be found in a little trading estate in Ancoat's. It is now run by two of the guys that were there when I started; they are Barry Loundsback and Chris Massey who bought the business from Gordon Hedley to allow Gordon to retire, although Barry and Chris must both be close to, if not past, retirement age by now.

THE YOUTH EMPLOYMENT OFFICE

My redundancy from Hedley's was followed by a visit to the Youth Employment Office at Deansgate, Manchester, where I was interviewed by an apathetic, haggard character dressed in an ill fitting, pin stripe suit which hung loosely from his Spartan frame. That civil servant, employed by the local authority, appeared unhealthily malnourished with his skeletal face and wispy, thinning, grey hair.

The plastic coated, wire framed spectacles which he wore looked like something that the NHS supplied to skenny eyed kids. The eye pieces bore thick lenses which resembled the bottoms of beer bottles. A cord, which was attached to the wire ear pieces, went around his scrawny, chicken like neck, and allowed the glasses to hang down to his chest so that they would not be misplaced.

Those spectacles which, when worn, made his eyes look unnaturally large, like ping pong balls that had an almost hypnotic effect, as they stared unblinkingly at me. The glasses were repeatedly put in place on his angular nose and then taken off again. When they were on he repeatedly pushed them up his long, thin, proboscis via his right index finger. When they were off he repeatedly wiped them with a handkerchief, which he clasped in the bony, claw like fingers of his left hand.

On a table before the Youth Employment Officer lay a bundle of papers, joined together at the top left hand corner by a thread that had been passed through the holes which had been punched through each page. That bundle of papers enclosed in a cardboard folder constituted my official file and what little there was of my work history to that day.

The interview began as soon as I was seated opposite him, across the table in a small interview cubicle. He smiled, showing a row of misshapen and crooked teeth, and then made a point of informing me that there were no vacancies within my chosen career in the printing trade. He then explained to me fully, the futility of pursuing my option in that vocation. The reason for this negativity was because he had a number of vacancies that he had to fill at Deansgate Parcel's Rail Depot for the positions of van lads and trailer boys. It was one of those positions that I was offered.

As the interviewer spoke he intermittently glanced at his watch and again pushed his spectacles up his beak like nose. It was at that point that I realised that I was something of an encumbrance to the man, a burden which he had, one way or another, to deal with. It seemed that he couldn't wait to be rid of me. What I had wanted was of no concern to him. What he had wanted was to see the innocent, ill prepared youth sat before him pushed into something that the he had not wanted to do, so as to fill the mundane vacancies that the clerk was charged to dispose of.

Those positions for the unskilled would be forced upon any other, poor, unsuspecting, unemployed adolescents that happened by that office for the unemployed juveniles of Manchester, until all the vacancies had been filled. It seemed to me that the Youth Employment Office was like a mass production facility with the youth of the day being the components on the conveyor belt of jobseekers.

That cadaverous looking civil servant who had features so sharp that he resembled a ravenous bird of prey, albeit a myopic, ravenous bird of prey, related to me what had to be done as he wrote out an introduction card with his gold nibbed, Conway Stewart, fountain pen which he held between the bony forefinger and thumb of his right, liver spotted hand. A hand which had shown every sinew and vein and was joined to a wrist that was no thicker than a baby's ankle.

The knuckles and joints of his hands were swollen and malformed as if through arthritis. In appearance he resembled a Victorian clerk, in the style of Dickens' Uriah Heep, hunched over a desk upon which rested a ledger in which he made entries with a feathered quill. This clerk, though, was not the obsequious, servile, fawning Uriah Heep, wringing his hands and mumbling 'Very 'umble.' He was a man with a purpose that no mere youth would stand in the way of. His sole purpose was to clear his books of all vacancies whether the applicant fitted the post or not.

As he spoke my eyes were transfixed to his very prominent Adam's apple which bobbed up and down with every syllable spoken. It was as if a large chunk of unswallowed food was caught in the conduit of his throat. Upon finishing his writing the sunken eyed, hollow cheeked, lath of a man handed to me the card to indicate that the interview was over and said, 'Here is a card of introduction for the position as a trailer boy at the Deansgate Parcels Rail Depot. The card is made out to an Inspector Ernest Etchells. Please be good enough to present Mr Etchells with this card and he will interview you for the said position. Off you go then young man and good luck.'

I said 'Thank you,' as I took the card from his bony, misshapen, taloned claw. I then left the Youth Employment Office and made my way across to Deansgate Parcels Rail Depot.

The depot was just across the road from the Youth Employment Office, the entrance being at the junction of Bridgewater Street and Watson Street, close to the Bridgewater Street railway bridge, which cast an ominous, long, black shadow over the entrance to the Deansgate Depot and which carried the lines into and out of Central Station. Watson Street ran parallel with Deansgate from Peter Street to Great Bridgewater Street.

DEANSGATE DEPOT

Trepidation caused me to hesitate at the gateway of Deansgate depot, anxious to know what was on the other side but, at the same time, dreading the unknown. In the shadows I waited, rotating the introduction card in my hands and gazing at it as if seeking guidance. A few minutes were taken considering my next action and taking in what I could see of the yard. It appeared dark and dingy; there was a funereal gloom which seemed tangible.

The black brick, perimeter wall was damp and the dark grey mortar, cracked and missing in places, was home to various invertebrate, exo-skeletal insects, arachnids and isopods and served as an anchor for the mosses, lichens and other growths that flourished there under damp, shady conditions. Even in the mid-afternoon of a sunny day it seemed cold and hostile, a most depressing and unfriendly place; so much so that I almost decided to turn my back on the depot and walk away.

But being filled with anxiety and yet with a strange desire, I stood for a few minutes more and watched numerous railway's liveried vehicles come and go through the wide, open, double, wooden gates. The minutes seemed like hours as they slowly passed and then, decidedly, I took a deep breath and strode purposely and resolutely through the open portal, on my voyage of discovery, into the dismal looking depot and into the world of British Rail.

The vehicles that had been watched and studied by my inquisitive eyes, as they passed in and out of the yard, were painted in the British Rail colours of maroon and cream, commonly known as the blood and custard livery. These colours could be seen on carriages of rolling stock and in railway stations and waiting rooms the length and breadth of the London, Midland Region.

Upon crossing the threshold my attention was drawn to a dim light emanating from the grimy, uncurtained window of a single storey, brick structure which occupied a position to the left of the gate, just a few yards into the depot. To the right of the entrance was a block end rail track with the buffers rusted solidly in the open position, the rails were coated with a red/brown oxidisation and were overgrown with brambles and weeds.

Alongside the track and abutting Watson Street there were numerous railway arches which were once used as stables and for storage. Those arches were, by then, left empty and unused except for the detritus that had been discarded or thrown into them and allowed to accumulate. They ran along the length of the disused track and parallel to the perimeter road, for the full length of the yard. Neither the track nor the arches had been used for several years and were home to large twitchy nosed rodents and other creepy crawlies. The roadway at this section was open to the elements, but as it made a circumference of the yard it entered the darkness beneath the upper yard which it supported.

In the middle of the yard was a raised loading deck, approximately one hundred yards long by twenty yards wide, and built around substantial supporting stanchions. Along both of its lengths were loading bays, approximately four feet from the floor. Some with vehicles backed on and others empty. Each loading bay had a shutter that could be lifted and lowered and locked into position. From the open loading bays shone a meagre light and from those that were closed light could be seen escaping from the base where the shutter met the floor.

At the corner of that loading deck, nearest to me, as I viewed it from the entrance to the depot, was a flight of five steps leading up to a door which allowed entrance to the loading bays. I found out later that the clocking on station and the clerks office was situated on the loading deck and also that there was a corresponding flight of steps diagonally opposite at the other end of the loading deck.

The yard itself was situated below the spurs and loops of the lines that ran into Manchester's Central Station. The whole yard supported Central Station's marshalling yard and as such had massive iron stanchions at approximately thirty feet intervals in all directions to supply this support. At the top end of the yard was the Great Northern Railway's Warehouse, situated a couple of blocks back from Peter Street and stretching from Watson Street to Deansgate. The warehouse had rail lines running into it from both upper and lower levels. Nowadays both upper and lower tiers of the yard are car parks and The Great Northern Railway Warehouse consists of coffee shops, bars, dineries and a multiplicity of retail outlets. Manchester Central Station became the G-Mex conference centre and exhibition hall and all the land belonging to the Railways' that lay adjacent and around Watson Street and Central Station is now used for car parking. New buildings have appeared where there were once rows of railway arches that were leased to small independent businesses. The G-Mex centre has recently been renamed and is once again called Manchester Central.

The brick building, which I had first noticed upon entering the yard and to the left of the entrance gates, once again, caught my attention and I walked towards it realising, as I did so, that the stables I had seen and the granite setts upon which I trod were throw backs to the not so long ago days of horse drawn vehicles.

As I approached and looked for the entrance to the small, cottage like, brick fabrication, it came to my notice that it was rather poorly maintained with decayed pointing and slipping slates. The entrance to this little house like building gave on to a little passage that ran the width of the building and had built into it a sliding communication hatch, which I supposed, quite rightly, was where the menials and minions conversed with the inspectors. In this passageway was a door which was painted in the railway's maroon, and was flaking and peeling. Upon it was screwed a tarnished brass sign declaring 'Inspector's Office.' It seemed pertinent to knock and so I rapped gently upon the door; a deep, slightly upper class Manchester accented voice responded with the single word 'Enter.'

The brass door knob was before me and so, tentatively, I turned it. It was in stark contrast to the tarnished sign above it, its shine being due to the friction of the many hands that had regularly opened and shut the door over a long period of time. Upon passing through the doorway, I was greeted with a cheery 'Hello, young man.' by the Inspector in charge, Mr Ernest Etchells.

Before replying, my eyes scanned the room, taking it all in. The internal walls and ceiling of this single roomed building, like the passageway, were daubed in the cream paint used extensively by the LM region of the railways. Stood against the back wall there was a small, cast iron, coal fired, pot bellied stove bearing a cast iron kettle whose lid was gently rising and falling as it calmly murmured and simmered away like a welcoming censer of hospitality. From its spout steam issued forth and rose to the ceiling where it condensed and occasionally dripped to the floor.

Next to the stove stood an iron coal scuttle and a shovel. It was in front of the stove that Inspector Etchells stood casually warming himself.

Taking up most space in that little office was a desk with a typewriter and various other railway's and administration paraphernalia. Lastly, sat on the table was a half drank mug of tea. There were two chairs, one situated at either side of the desk. In one corner was a filing cabinet cum storage cupboard next to which was a coat and hat stand. The last fitment in this little room was a small hand basin fitted with a single cold water tap. There was no toilet adjoined to this inspector's bungalow, it seemed that the inspector had to use the communal toilets across the yard for his ablutions, as per the lowly workers, although the inspectors W.C. could only be accessed by way of a key.

Inspector Etchells was one of two inspectors that ran Deansgate depot. The other being a gentleman by the name of Harold Carroll, who worked the opposing shift. Inspector Etchells was the senior of the two. He was slightly more than six feet tall, with thinning, grey, wavy hair. He was dressed in the Inspector's uniform which consisted of a black blazer over a waistcoat which camouflaged his slight paunch. Attached to the waistcoat, by way of a silver, double Albert watch chain, was a large railway's timepiece. The chain carried the key for the watch. Beneath the waistcoat he wore a white shirt with detachable collar under which was fastened, with a neat Windsor knot, a railway's tie. The dark grey trousers that he wore had razor sharp creases. On top of all this he wore a long Railway's great coat. His black leather, Oxford shoes were buffed to a mirror finish; he was, in essence, a shining example of the epitome of corporate, sartorial elegance.

'Hello sir' I said in response to his greeting as I offered him the card from the Youth Employment Office. I then informed him of my name and the reason I had paid him this visit. He in turn offered me a seat and explained to me what was required of a trailer boy cum van lad and of what the job consisted. He said, 'My name, young fellow, is Inspector Ernest Etchells and this depot is designated a passenger, parcels depot, which means, young man, that we only deliver and collect goods of a size that can be carried on passenger trains, in the guards van usually, or other covered rolling stock that constitutes an express parcels train. You, young un', will be known as a driver's nipper, which is railway's parlance for a van lad/trailer boy. Your tasks will be to ably assist your driver in the preparing and the loading and unloading of his vehicle and the delivery of boxes, cartons, cases, chests, crates, envelopes, packages, parcels and trunks on a dedicated delivery round. You may also be called upon to deliver various items of livestock, usually of the domesticated type, such as cats, dogs, fish, the occasional farm breeds and now and again animals, birds and reptiles of a more exotic nature there may be perishable goods such as foodstuffs, flowers, fruits and vegetables of all kinds. There may also be certain medical supplies that may have to be delivered.'

'You will, if you take the post on offer, work, on a day shift, with a roundsman until you are eighteen years of age when you will go on to shift work. At eighteen years of age you may apply for the railway's, road vehicle, driving school, when, if you pass, young Driver you will become a young driver on shift work. If you fail you will be offered a porter's position. You can apply for the driving school up to three times. If you fail three times there are still a host of other jobs within the railway's businesses that you can apply for, be they manual or clerical.'

'I notice from your introduction card that you have a number of GCE's. This is most unusual, if not unknown, for the post of a trailer boy and I would suggest that you try to avail yourself of a clerical position later as this may suit your education somewhat better. Before all this can come to fruition, young fellow, you will first have to pass the railway's medical examination, which

I shall arrange for you. So what do you think? Is this the job for you, young man?'

'If I pass the medical I would like to give it a shot, sir, if that's O.K.'? I replied, not quite sure that I was making the right decision.

'Certainly, my boy; write your name and address on this card and then leave it to me and expect a letter shortly for your medical appointment. Now off you go and I'm sure we will meet again in the near future. Good bye for now.'

After I had written all my details in the space provided on the introduction card and handed it back to the Inspector I replied 'Good bye, Inspector Etchells, for now.' And with that I took my leave.

The medical was arranged. I attended and passed it without any problems as I was then a fit young man who took regular exercise. I was given a date to start work at Deansgate Parcels Depot. The job was one that I considered just about suitable for a trained monkey, but I had committed myself and I thought it would do until, maybe, something a little more suitable came along. I was grossly mistaken.

THE LONDON MIDLAND REGION

The London Midland Region (LMR) was one of the six regions set up on the formation of the nationalised British Rail (BR) in 1948 by Clement Attlee's Labour Government and consisted of ex London, Midland and Scottish Railway (LMS) lines in England and Wales. The region was first managed from London Euston but later the running of the region was undertaken from Stanier House in Birmingham.

The London Midland Region existed from the creation of BR in 1948. It ceased to be an operating unit in its own right in the

1980's and was wound up in 1992. The LMR's territory consisted of the ex LMS lines in England and Wales, except for lines East of Skipton in Yorkshire. The LMS lines running through Scotland became part of the Scottish region. The Mersey Railway, which had avoided being 'Grouped' with the LMS in 1923, also joined the London Midland Region. The other regions formed at the same time as the London Midland were the Eastern Region, The North Eastern Region, The Southern Region, The Western Region and the Scottish Region.

The principal territory covered by the London Midland Region consisted of the West Coast Main Line, (WCML) and the Midland Main Line (MML) south of Carlisle and the ex-Midland Cross Country Route from Bristol to Leeds.

INTRODUCTION AND INDUCTION TO BR

My new employment started two weeks after my interview at 08.00hrs on a Monday morning. Upon arriving at the depot I made the acquaintance of two other new recruits. We each had over our shoulders a brown workman's haversack and each of us clutched a white enamelled metal brew can. My haversack contained all the ingredients for the making of tea and coffee plus a sandwich that my mother had prepared for my dinner. I felt like a proper little railwayman.

Our first day was an induction day. We were given time cards and shown where to clock on. We were then introduced to the drivers that we would be working with the following day and probably, if we were to stick it out, until we were eighteen years of age. The driver who I was to assist on the round upon which I was to be a trailer boy was a man named Jake Barlow and his round covered the Manchester areas of Hulme, Knott Mill, Gaythorn, Whitworth Park and part of Chorlton on Medlock.

Jake as it turned out, was only a dozen years my senior, but to a sixteen year old youth anyone who had passed twenty years of age was considered old and anyone over twenty five years of age was positively ancient.

Once the introductions were out of the way we were taken to the British Rail offices at Hunt's Bank, near Victoria Station. There we were measured for our uniforms and issued with the closest approximation to our measurements.

The rest of that first day was spent learning a little about the passenger railways and its history starting with the fact that the first permanent steam railway for passengers was the Stockton to Darlington line which was inspired by a wealthy wool merchant named Edward Pease (1767-1850), and that the Stockton and Darlington Railway (S&DR); was authorised by parliament in 1821.The S&DR was inaugurated on the twenty fifth of September 1825 and was built by George Stephenson. Its original design was for a horse drawn, plateway, but Stephenson who had been perfecting his steam driven locomotive, petitioned Parliament and got his way to build a permanent way to carry his steam propelled engine.

This new railway which was initially built to link inland coal mines to Stockton on Tees used the four feet, eight and one half inch gauge, so as to accommodate the numerous horse drawn wagons, of that gauge, which served the coal mines. This gauge later became the British standard rail gauge. On the day it was opened, provision was made for three hundred passengers to travel but up to six hundred individuals actually made their way on to the train.

Other topics covered on that induction day were health and safety in the workplace, the BR pension, our pay scale and our right to union membership plus holiday entitlements. We were given catalogues showing many and various types of safety footwear which were recommended but not supplied by the BR.

Safety footwear, in those days before political correctness and prior to the importance of Health and Safety in the Workplace was universally recognised, had to be purchased by the worker. Nowadays it is the responsibility of the company to supply all 'Personal Protective Equipment.'

We learnt about the free and subsidised travel that we would be entitled to after serving three months with the company. These entitlements improved with length of service until employees with the requisite amount of service could avail themselves and their immediate family members, of free or subsidised rail travel across the European continent and even further afield.

British Rail had a reciprocative arrangement with railway companies abroad which allowed such travel. Elder, senior railwaymen and those with years on the job, travelled far and wide, with their families, under this agreement. The lowly van lad or trailer boy used his concessions for day trips to Blackpool with his mates.

We were released from duty at approximately 1500hrs that day and told to report back for duty at 0800hrs the following morning.

The following day I arrived at the depot early, neatly dressed in my railwayman's uniform, comprising of a grey jacket and trousers, a long sleeved, black waistcoat of which we were issued two, a railway's grey, cotton shirt and tie of which we were issued three, a railway's full length, black barathea great coat of which we received one every two years, all crowned off with a peaked railway hat adorned with the LM Region's badge. Rolled up in my haversack was a pair of company issue overalls. I felt even more like a proper little railwayman.

At the clocking on station I met the other two new starters who were dressed identically to myself and were carrying their white enamel brew cans with haversacks slung across their bodies' bandoleer style. Inspector Etchells was at the clocking on station, apparently waiting for us new employees and he directed us to the mess room to find our nominated drivers. As we approached the door to the mess room, we heard a medley of discordant voices, a hubbub of noise. Individual words were not quite decipherable from this disharmonious clamour although it was obviously the sound of numerous human conversations.

Tentatively, I reached for the latch of the door and swung it outwards. The sight that greeted us new recruits was one of utter chaos and disorder with people milling about and others sat at tables eating and drinking. Yet other tables were given over to gambling with large amounts of coinage and some notes forming the kitties of which ever card game was being played. It seemed reminiscent of a western saloon with cowboys of a different kind. Smoke, from numerous cigarettes, hung in the air in stratas of blue and grey, being joined by ever rising swirls of freshly blown or drifting smoke. It was what I supposed a Chinese opium den full of the retching and coughing of numerous addicts might be like.

The mess room itself was a large, dingy, brick building that bore the appearance of converted stables. Through its length it was split into two rooms with an arch way between them. Each segment contained numerous chairs and tables and each had a pot bellied, coal fed stove with a blackened, metal chimney protruding through the ceiling to take away the noxious fumes.

Hanging from the ceiling, in each half, was a dim, lit, naked light bulb, held by a flex which, like the dangling orb of meagre luminescence, was stained brown by the nicotine and smoke. A kerosene or candlelit, wagon wheel, chandelier, suspended on chains from the ceiling, would not have looked out of place in this smoke filled, quasi Western, gambling den and may have just cast a little more light than the electrical fittings that were in place.

The windows to the rear were begrimed and be-sooted with the residues from the pot bellied stoves mixed with the tar and nicotine of years of accumulated tobacco smoke and could be barely seen through. Each half of the mess room contained a large, copper, hot water geyser positioned next to a draining board that directed any spillage or overflow into a large, brown, stoneware, Belfast sink that was almost big enough to bathe in.

As we stood at the door prior to entering, a voice from somewhere within the room hollered 'Shut that fuckin' door!' We walked through the door and closed it behind us. Jake looked up from his game of cards, picked me out from the other entrants and beckoned me over, 'Get yourself a brew while I finish this game of cards.' he told me. I nodded my acceptance and made my way to the hot water geyser followed by the other new lads, who had been given the same instructions by their drivers.

Whilst traversing the room towards the boiler we were jostled, pushed, and manhandled, we were also subjected to verbal abuse, but we finally made it to the brew station where we filled our brew cans and tried to make ourselves as inconspicuous as possible Our attempt to blend into the décor and immediate surroundings, dressed, as we were, in brand new railway uniforms and carrying pristinely white brew cans and unstained haversacks over our shoulders was doomed to failure. We stood out like the proverbial sore thumb.

[1]As we reached the water geyser and before filling our brew cans, there was an elderly driver, whose name, I later found out was, Harold Richards, filling his ancient and battered brew can. Upon finishing this operation he turned around into a relatively empty space where he started to swing the brew can back and forth to mix the brew. Each arc became larger with every swing until he was swinging it full circle. Those closest to him moved away and enough space opened up around him to allow for this

---

1. A fuller account of this incident can be found in the earlier book 'This Trucking' Life

operation. During one of the rotations, the chipped can and its contents parted company with its handle and like a stone from a slingshot flew across the room trailing boiling tea in its wake. It came to a sudden halt as it hit one of the card players on the back of the head, depositing what remained of its contents down his back. There was a verbal onslaught of impious profanity and the card player, an Irish guy named Mick, rose and looked around to ascertain from whence the offending object had begun its journey. His eyes, squinting through a red mist, fell upon the elderly driver who was gazing, in utter bewilderment, at his hand which still tightly clutched the brew can handle.

The offended driver, with steam rising from his back and shoulders like the foggy vapours of a morning mist in a lowland glen, threw off his great coat and stepped towards the older guy, bunched his fist and in his rage threw a wild punch. This haymaker went wide of the mark and a couple of drivers stepped between the pair to stop any further assault. Anger subsided, apologies were offered and accepted, hands were shaken and things returned to a semblance of normality.

The driver that had been subjected to the force of the tea charged missile, had upon his frame, each and every layer of his uniform and was well insulated from the dregs of the scalding infusion and but for the lump on his head and the sudden shock that he received, he was relatively unscathed.

Some of the drivers and their lads that were in the mess room at the time had started at what I considered an unearthly hour. That hour being 0530 and what we were witnessing was their tea-break or breakfast time.

After the confrontation between Mick and Harold, had been quelled; I was conversing with my new acquaintances, when I felt a tap on my shoulder. I slowly turned around, dreading what would be there to greet me and with fear in my eyes, to be confronted by Jake who was beaming widely and finding great amusement in my introduction to BR's; pre duty and early social activities. He asked, with amusement in his voice 'Are you ready? We'll go and load up and get going. My truck's already backed onto the bay so I'll show you what to do. Come on.'

'Yeah, sure, I'm as ready as I'll ever be, let's go.' Was my reply, uttered with rather more confidence than I actually felt.

Jake led the way, chuckling to himself as I followed him out of the mess room and to the loading deck spilling my tea as I went. We reached the loading deck and climbed the steps and entered the raised area and made our way to Jake's bay where the open shutter of his trailer yawned gapingly at us. Following my driver's instructions I clambered down from the loading bay and stowed my gear in the cab of the Scammell Scarab which was hooked up to the trailer. I then climbed back onto the deck and we proceeded to load up the trailer with that day's deliveries. Jake instructed me how to load and stack the outgoing parcels and packages in drop order for ease of delivery. We then jumped off the loading bay to ground level and my driver then taught me how to perform the daily checks of the vehicle; oil, water, fuel, tyres etc.

The oil was checked via an external dipstick and if necessary the oil filler cap was removed and the unctuous liquid poured into the engine to bring it to the required level and not, as in a story that Jake related to me how one of his previous trailer boys had attempted to top up the engine lubricant by trying to pour the oil down the ¼ inch hole where the dipstick rested. That attempt resulted in *oleum* spilling over the engine and dripping to the floor directly beneath the vehicle which the lad then had to clean up. The youngster never made that mistake again.

The water was checked by unscrewing the filler cap and gazing down into the filler pipe. If water was visible it was okay, if not it had to be replenished. There was no fuel gauge in the primitive Scammell Scarab so to ascertain how much derv was in the tank the filler cap was removed and a dipstick was used to measure the amount of fuel on board. The tyres were firstly given a visual examination, then, if any doubt the steel toe capped, pressure gauge was employed. All the tyres were given a hefty kick to ascertain an approximation of their roadworthiness.

Jake's vehicle was a three tons, urban articulated vehicle, known as the Scammell Scarab, mechanical horse. It was a three wheeled unit which could turn in its own length and was powered by a 1.6 litre Perkins diesel engine. It was adjoined to the trailer by way of a superficial imposition known as Scammell's automatic, quick release coupling. It was a later version of the type of vehicle which had been brought in, years before, to replace the horse drawn trailers.

The trailer was of the box type with a single axle bearing a single wheel on each side, to the rear and was only sixteen to eighteen feet long. Loading was through the rear end of the trailer, which had a roller shutter which came ¾'s of way down the opening to join a tail board. That tailboard could be lowered so that it hung down or could be suspended on chains.

The only other type of articulated vehicle used at Deansgate Depot was the Karrier Bantam. They were four wheeled, light weight tractor units produced by Karrier Motors of Huddersfield which was part of the Roote's group. They were fitted with a similar, proprietary, automatic coupling which was totally compatible with Scammell's own.

Roundsmen who did domestic mail order deliveries and stores deliveries only and didn't have to reverse into the very tight loading bays of the factories of the day had rigid vehicles manufactured in the late 1940's and early 50's. The vehicles used were the 6 cylinder; petrol engined Bedford 'O' & 'K' types; 4D four cylinder Fordson Thames, powered by a 3.6 litre diesel or Ford's petrol engine. There were also Austin's and Morris' with 3.5 litre petrol engines and also a number of Dennis' with the 4.25, Rolls-Royce petrol engine or the Perkins's diesel. In about 1966 the TK Bedford was introduced, this was powered by Bedford's 330D diesel engine and was in production from 1960 until 1984. That was when petrol powered vehicles were being phased out to standardise on diesel power. It was around that time, when the TK Bedford was introduced, that the railway's in-house road transport became known as National Carriers Limited, (NCL). I remember that because, as I recall, the TK was the first vehicle to arrive at Deansgate Depot painted in the yellow livery of NCL. Other vehicles that were introduced to the parcels fleet when it became NCL were the Commer walk-through delivery van and the Bedford walk through delivery van which were of similar design and were perfect for parcel delivery because there was an entrance behind the drive that led directly into the load space. Lastly the Scammell Townsman was introduced. The Townsman was the latest update of the mechanical horse.

When I was introduced to Jake I also made the acquaintance of his then van lad 'Knocker' who's full name was Norman Hocker. Knocker and I became close friends and remained so. I replaced Knocker as Jake's trailer boy, because Knocker, having turned eighteen years of age, moved onto shifts or turns as they were called on the railways. Under Jake's instruction Norman had applied to go to the Railway's Road Vehicle Driving School prior to his eighteenth birthday and within a week of leaving Jake he was sent to the driving school at Hollinwood, a borough of Oldham. After six weeks intensive training he passed his test and returned to Deansgate as a fully fledged Railway's Road Vehicle Driver on shift work. His wages increased accordingly to the driver's rate of £ 9.10s (£9.50) per 42 hour week. That plus his shift payment and the fact that he could then work overtime placed him in, what we believed at the time to be, the high earners bracket. That, in a nutshell, was my introduction to working life on the railway.

CHAPTER 2
MECHANICAL HORSES

The Scammell mechanical horse was the stalwart and preferred unit within the railways and other companies as a local delivery vehicle from the day it was first introduced in the UK in 1932.

The railway companies, from the late 1920's, had been looking for a vehicle to replace the horse drawn carriages on local deliveries within municipal areas. One of the Southern rail companies approached a quality builder of auto and aero engines named Napier's. Napier's design engineers came up with a few designs but ultimately it was Scammell Lorries, utilising some of Napier's designs, which came through with a working Mechanical Horse designed by O.D. North. One of its unique design features was the Scammell Automatic Coupling which enabled coupling and uncoupling of trailers automatically.

The original Mechanical Horse was a large three wheeled tractor unit with a wooden cab built around a steel frame and came as either a three tonner or a six tonner. At the time Scammell's own engines were used. The three ton vehicle was powered by a 1,125cc engine and the six ton vehicle by a 2,045cc engine; both were petrol powered side valve engines. The original Scammell mechanical horse had canvas doors which could be rolled up and secured with a strap and a split windscreen that opened forwards on the driver's side.

Because this was the period of changeover from horse drawn vehicles to petroleum powered vehicles and because this period was a somewhat protracted affair, some engineer of vast ingenuity, devised a fitment that allowed the horse drawn carriages to couple up to the petrol powered prime mover, giving the best of both worlds.

Because of its three wheeled design, which gave it never before known manoeuvrability, it was ideal for delivery work. It could turn through 360 degrees in eighteen feet when coupled to a sixteen feet trailer. The Scammell Mechanical Horse remained largely unchanged until the late 1940's when the Scammell Scarab was introduced. This newly designed model had a steel cab, replaced by a fibre glass cab in the 1960's, and a much rounder front aspect. The engine was mounted lower, giving greater stability than the taller earlier designs.

Both the three & six tonners were fitted with Scammell's 2,090cc side valve engine. Later a diesel engine was introduced for each vehicle. The three tonner being powered by a 1,600cc Perkins' diesel engine and the six tonner vehicle powered by the Perkins' 3,140cc engine which was later superseded by their 3,330cc engine.

The companies that employed the use of the Scammell Scarab, besides all the railway companies, were numerous and varied and included The Royal Mail/GPO, BRS Parcels, Watney's Brewery, Calico Printers, BTP Cocker Chemicals Ltd; Selfridges of London, Eskimo Frozen Foods, United Glass, Skellingthorpe Saw Mills of Lincoln and many more including the armed forces. They were even used on aircraft carriers.

The Mechanical Horse was also developed as a long and a short wheel based rigid vehicle and many city and borough councils used the mechanical horse in its many guises because of its manoeuvrability for town work. It was used as a road sweeper or refuse collection vehicle. It was also fitted out as a fire engine by some authorities. Scammell marketed its rigid versions of the Mechanical Horse under the name 'Tri-Van'. Two were used, in the Blackwall Tunnel, one on the South side and one on the North, as rigid breakdown vehicles. They were the preferred vehicle because they could turn full circle within the confines of the tunnel.

Specialised trailers were developed for use with the tractor units with the Scammell Automatic Coupling; these took the form of gully emptiers and other tankers, drop side trailers, drop frame trailers, trailers for transporting sheet glass, insulated trailers for the carriage of frozen foodstuffs, extendable (trombone) trailers, exhibition trailers and standard box and flat bed trailers, some with a longer wheel base and chassis than that used by British Rail and other nationalised companies.

The Scammell Scarab was produced until 1967 and then was replaced by the Scammell Townsman which had a more aerodynamic, streamlined, fibreglass cab fitted with twin headlights; it had vacuum assisted, hydraulic brakes which, at the time, were only seen on larger, heavier motors. The Scammell Automatic Coupling mechanism was retained but was much improved with a vacuum operated trailer release button rather than the manual hand lever found in the earlier models.

A heater/demister became standard as did internal sun visors, larger mirrors and better signalling, better mpg; and faster travelling speed. Despite the many improvements the Townsman had over the Scarab it was mainly bought by the rail companies and the Royal Mail and production ceased in 1968.

In France, at the time, a vehicle called the FAR was built on license from Scammell. It was built by the French company of Chenard-Walker and was powered by the Citroen Traction Avant engine and again used the same coupling device. As well as Scammell and FAR numerous and various commercial truck makers used the Scammell Automatic Coupling mechanism on their smaller urban delivery vehicles, bringing them into the fold of the Mechanical Horse.

Karrier used a similar coupling on their small four wheeled tractor units the Cob and the Bantam of which the rail companies purchased numerous. Karrier manufactured its own coupling which was fully compatible with Scammell's. Earlier Karriers were fitted with petrol engines from the Rootes' factory but were later replaced by the Leyland OE160 diesel engine.

Jensen Motors of which the rail companies used numerous four wheel rigid models also produced a mechanical horse known as the Jen Tug which was a battery-electric powered truck. There were a number of experimental battery-electric tractor units placed in service to compare and compete with the Scammell Scarab such as the Austin/Crompton Parkinson 2.5 ton Battery-electric mechanical horse. The rail companies also bought those.

Ford Motors also produced a tractor unit as a mechanical horse. This unit was based on the Ford Y, model eight, car with automatic coupling; although I believe there was limited production of this model.

Thorneycroft, later known for their 'Mighty Antar' tank transporters was another vehicle maker that the rail companies seemed to have a lot of faith in. BRS also ran a Large number of Thorneycroft's. This company of vehicle makers developed the Thorneycroft 'Nippy' using the Scammell coupling; it was powered by a 4 litre engine.

Bedford TK's were also fitted with the Scammell coupling. The rail companies ran them with twenty eight feet trailers with a gross weight of twenty tons. Seddon and Dodge also did variations of the mechanical horse concept, utilising the Scammell coupling.

The larger four wheeled tractor units were used on town to town deliveries where a drop trailer system could be operated. The smaller three wheeled units were kept on local urban and suburban deliveries.

Reliant produced a mini mechanical horse in the late 1960's, designated the TW9 (three wheeled), it had a payload of only 16cwt and used Reliant's 750cc engine. The design was taken up by Dunn BTB and called the Ant. Most were of the pick up type although one example of this machine as an artic still survives. Production of this vehicle was farmed out to Greece and Turkey.

The Scammell Automatic Coupling itself consisted of two ramps adjoined to the unit chassis with hooks placed forward of the rear wheels. There was a striker plate for raising the jockey wheels on the trailer. The trailer had an undercarriage mounted under its front end which equates to the turntable on a fifth wheel equipped vehicle.

The undercarriage had two roller wheels which, as the unit was reversed under the trailer, rolled up the ramps. The lower part of the undercarriage terminated with the Jockey wheels which as the rollers ran up the ramps, folded back when the striker plate was struck. The hooks at the end of the ramps engaged with lugs on the trailer making a secure engagement with the unit. The trailer brake and trailer light connections were made automatically, leaving the driver with just the trailer number plate to fit and the trailer hand brake, which is on a ratcheted quadrant at the front of the trailer, to release.

One fault with this type of coupling is that the driver, if not taking adequate care, could pull away too fast when dropping the trailer, not allowing enough time for the trailer legs to descend and thus dropping the trailer on its knees. Carelessness of this sort could cause extensive damage to the trailer undercarriage and the front end of the trailer. This was actually more of a driver fault than a design fault and a number of drivers were reprimanded for their carelessness when dropping trailers.

There exists a Mechanical Horse club where enthusiasts can get together and meet. The club is responsible for restoration projects and finding old vehicles that can still be restored and it also does a lot of work in keeping a very important part of our transport heritage alive. The club membership consists of individuals and groups. One such group, although now disbanded was a body of men from the Manchester area referred to as the 'Famous Five' gang.

I knew all of the five who were: Charlie Warner with whom I worked at Deansgate Parcels Depot where Charles was once a driver; rumour has it that he was originally employed as a rodent catcher. He was promoted to a foreman's position and later transferred to Longsight Freightliner Terminal and then Trafford Park FLT; as a supervisor.

Next there was John 'Bebby' Bebbington who started on the railway as a chain horse boy at London Road and later became a driver. He later transferred to Freightliner where he worked as a driver at both Longsight and Trafford Park Terminals. Johnny Hayes was a driver at Edgeley, Stockport before becoming a British Rail Driving Instructor. He then transferred to Trafford Park, Freightliner, as a supervisor, where I knew him. The fourth in this group was Malcolm Ruscoe who I only knew as a passing acquaintance. He worked at Oldham Road Goods Depot before transferring to Manchester, Trafford Park. The last of the Famous Five is Dennis Alty. Dennis was a plant engineer at The Manchester, Trafford Park Terminal and was someone that I knew but did not have a lot to do with at the time. The above mentioned railwaymen are now retired and since retirement they have restored a three ton Scammell Scarab Mechanical Horse and its semi trailer to its former glory. This fully restored vehicle looks resplendent in its blood and custard livery.

The Mechanical Horse Club is run on a national basis and has members all over the British Isles. It doesn't deal only with the Scammell Scarab, but has an interest in all the many and varied vehicles that use the Scammell Automatic Coupling, including the original Scammell mechanical Horse that was introduced in 1932. It is the use of the Scammell Automatic Coupling that brings these vehicles under the umbrella term 'Mechanical Horse.'

CHAPTER 3
A DAY IN THE LIFE OF A
YOUNG TRAILER BOY

After learning the sequence of loading and checking the vehicle over Jake and I proceeded on our first day out working together. Once loaded we left the yard and headed for Aston's café on Cambridge street, opposite The Dunlop Rubber Company. This was actually on Jake's round, but we met four or five other drivers and their van lads there. The drivers that we met were Jake's closest buddies at the depot. There was Albert Shaw who delivered around the Wythenshawe area, Billy McMahon whose round was also part of the Wythenshawe area. Billy's van lad was a youth from Chorlton cum Hardy named Kevin Clarke or Clarkie as he became known. I only mention Clarkie by name because he is the only van lad whose name I remember from those days at Aston's café.

There was Albert de Toper who delivered to the parts of Hulme that Jake's round did not take in plus Brook's Bar, Moss Side and Old Trafford. Bob Hoey and Phil Weatherhilt also joined us at Aston's for breakfast where the drivers, as a matter of course, paid for their mate's breakfasts.

The Café belonged to the elder brother of footballer John Aston. John Aston played for Manchester United in the 50's and was in the 1950 World Cup Squad. One of his sons also called John played for United in the 1960's. Young John is now a retailer owning a shop, which I believe his father owned before him, in Stalybridge, near Manchester.

After our morning repast the deliveries would be undertaken. Some of the companies on Jake's round were Dunlop Rubber, The Hotspur Press, Odhams Press, The Daily Sketch Press, DOT Motorcycle Factory and The Manchester Poster Services which made posters for cinemas, William Pownall's Carpets, Selas Gas and the Salvation Army depot plus others and a whole host of domestic and shop deliveries.

On Jake's delivery round was the Clinic for Sexually Transmitted Diseases better known as the VD clinic which at the time was on Duke Street, just off Liverpool Road. Jake seemed to be embarrassed about going into this place and would make me take any deliveries in. When I came out through the patients door empty handed, after having made the delivery Jake would say loud enough for any passers by to hear, 'Hey, you've stopped scratching. Is it cured now?' This caused me quite a lot of embarrassment, but I got used to Jake's bit of fun.

There were also two railway stations on Jake's round that we had to deliver to on various occasions. The nearest one to the depot was Knott Mill station, now known as Deansgate Railway station. The station building is a grade two listed building and lies to the South of the city near to the Castlefield area.

Knott Mill Station was originally opened in1849 and the original station buildings were wooden. Because the wooden buildings were considered an eyesore it was decided to pull them down and acquire some adjacent land to build the new station. The rebuilding was finished in 1896. The Station became Knott mill And Deansgate around 1900 and finally Deansgate in 1971.

The other station on the round was Oxford Road station which was first constructed during the building of South Junction Line viaduct which opened in 1849.Between 1958 and 1960 the station was extensively rebuilt to coincide with the 25kV electrification of the railway from Piccadilly (then called London Road). It was during this time that the old station building was demolished to make way for the then ultra modern wood and glass structure that took its place. That 'new' building which still stands has become a grade two listed building.

Jake was adept at reversing his little articulated vehicle into loading bays that were made for horses and carts, as I watched in amazement, not believing that I would soon be capable of doing the same. He reversed the vehicle and trailer onto and into loading bays, using just his mirrors for guidance, when the loading bays were only a couple of inches wider than the trailer.

When the morning's deliveries were completed we would return to the depot or any other of the numerous canteens for dinner. After dinner we would go out and do a number of collections which would be brought back to the depot for sorting for destinations further afield. After unloading the collection of parcels that we had brought into the depot, it was then end of the working day for the driver's mate who would clock off and go home.

The driver, for overtime, would do a trip to Knightsbridge Bakery at Ayres Road, Old Trafford, with either another driver or a shift working van lad. Once loaded at Knightsbridge the load would be delivered and off loaded at Mayfield or Victoria station for sorting for destinations all over the nation before the driver and mate returned to Deansgate to park up, complete any paperwork and to get clocked off. This was the usual working day and what I could look forward to until I reached 18 years of age when I would either go on shifts as a trailer boy or porter or, with luck, go to the driving school.

I worked with Jake until I was eighteen. He was a pleasure to work with. He rarely took any of the gratuities that we were offered choosing to let me keep them all. The only time he took a share was at Christmas time which was only fair because some of the firms gave up to a fiver and/or a bottle of whisky or other spirits. Jake was a man of principle and as such he impressed upon me the need for respect and integrity within the workplace and gave me a sense of values within the railway structure.

CANTEENS & COMMON SENSE

All the rail depots around the Manchester area had their own subsidised canteens which, at the time were staffed by railway personnel. Some canteens were better than others and drivers had their favourites. Deansgate Depot was no exception to the rule. It had its own canteen which was housed on the second floor of the building that fronted onto Deansgate. The ground floor of this building, which belonged to the railway, was rented or leased out to various retail outlets. Most of them, at the time were motorcycle shops or motorcycle accessory shops. The top floor was rented or leased out as office space to various companies.

One dinner time myself, Knocker and another van boy named Mitch decided that we would grace the canteen with our presence. There was a back entrance from the depot yard which we used. This entrance was accessed via the buildings fire escape. Upon reaching the canteen we found that business was brisk and that the canteen was almost full, not with railway staff of which there were a few, I hasten to add, but with office workers and shop staff from around the Deansgate area.

The area of the canteen that we normally used, which was close to the serving area and had bare tables, was totally full. We waited, watching for people that had finished their meals and that were about to leave. After about 5 minutes waiting we managed to obtain possession of a table as it was vacated and plonked ourselves down. The table, which one of the canteen staff cleared of used crockery etc; had a white linen cloth covering it and a half empty carafe of water in the centre. We went for our meals one at a time to ensure that we would not lose the table. When all three of us were sat dining the canteen manager approached, dressed in his very neat, work attire and sporting a French style, waxed moustache and looking somewhat incensed. 'What do you think you are doing sitting here?' He asked in a voice raised in pitch so that everybody could hear him and so as to cause us some embarrassment.

'We're having our dinners.' I replied, stating the blindingly obvious.

'Well, you can't sit here dressed in dirty labourer's overalls,' he said 'these tables are reserved for office staff, hence the linen.' This was spoken slightly louder for an enhanced effect. His statement though was not accurate as we were all neatly and cleanly attired; we wore uniforms and not overalls. To this officious prat we were a totally different breed to the office staff for which these tables with their white linen and carafes were intended. To him we were not worthy or deserving of these dining positions.

As this conversation was being carried on Jake entered the canteen and heard what was going on and before I could reply I heard Jake say to the canteen manager, 'What have we here then? Is this a case of class distinction in a railwayman's canteen? These boys have been out working all morning for the LM region of the railways and it is now time for their well deserved repast. They work for the railway and this is a railway canteen and dining area, and I heard you say that these tables are reserved for office staff. By whom are these office staff employed? Are they railway personnel? If not, are they to be better accommodated in a railway canteen than railway employees? If so are they to be afforded better service than their manual counterparts? I sincerely think not, my man.'

With each question and comment Jake made the canteen manager appeared to pale and shrink into insignificance, his once confident manner had deserted him. He stuttered as he attempted to respond to Jake's barrage. 'Bu, bu, bu, but…'

'No buts about it!' Jake exclaimed 'this canteen is almost full and these lads took the only table available, where I am about to join them. Would you like to see them go without a midday meal because of your petty rules or should I take it up with a higher authority?' Perhaps you would like to tell me that I cannot sit here because I am dressed in a driver's uniform. Or is it that you think you represent the face of authority and you can bully these young fellows?' All this was said without raising his voice but, nevertheless, conferring menace.

Finding his tongue, at last, the manager said in a grovelling, subservient manner, as he bowed and reversed away from the source of his growing dilemma, 'I didn't mean to cause any problems, I am terribly sorry, please,.......... feel free to join your companions; I will see to it that your carafe is refilled.' With that he turned around rather quickly and almost knocked over a customer who was making his way to another table carrying a tray of food. He was forced to issue another apology before beating a hasty retreat to the refuge of his office.

The dining room had gone deathly quiet throughout this somewhat one sided exchange and as the manager made his way back towards his office via the cooking area he was subjected to all manner of taunts and asides as conversation began to slowly fill the room once again.

Jake then joined the queue for his victuals where he was congratulated by one of the female serving staff on his handling of the situation with 'That jumped up little pipsqueak of a Jobsworth.' as she called the canteen manager. Jake returned to the table with his comestibles and sat down to eat. As he did so one of the dinner ladies appeared at the table with a carafe of fresh water and four glasses. She placed her hand on Jack's shoulder and said 'Well done. The little prat deserved that.' We thanked Jake for his fortuitous appearance in the canteen and his intervention on our behalf and we all shared a laugh about it.

The next time we used the canteen; all the tables were covered with white linen, and lowly van lads and trailer boys were afforded the same courtesies as everyone else. A good day for common sense thanks to Jake. The canteen manager kept a very low profile whenever Jake appeared.

THE STUPIDITY OF YOUTH

Because dinner time on the railway often stretched to two hours, some days a bunch of van lads and perhaps some of the drivers would go swimming at the public swimming baths within Sunlight House, which was on Quay Street, just off Deansgate or maybe they would join in the football game which was regularly played in the yard, or even just have dinner in the canteen and spend the rest of the time lounging around. But during my first summer of working at Deansgate Rail Depot and being of that age where youthful exuberance, fearlessness, foolishness and a propensity for being completely stupid seemed to be contained in equal amounts, I and some other youths committed a quite senseless and out of the ordinary act.

As mentioned in the prior few paragraphs there was a back entrance to the canteen which was accessed via an external fire escape which led to the roof of the building and on one summer's day of that first summer on the railways, we youths, Knocker, Mitch, Jimmy Mac and me, because we were bored and inquisitive, climbed to the roof to take the sun.

Once on the roof which had a slight apex and valley gutters which were lined with lead, we started to explore. Jimmy Mac said, 'Ey, look at dese lead lined gutters. Lead's about free quid an 'undredweight yuh know, an' dere's tons of it up 'ere an' ah can get mi 'ands under dis piece an' pull it up.' and he promptly attempted to do just that. The rest of us joined in the tug o' war with a six feet length of heavy duty, lead sheet which was about two feet wide and pointed into the brickwork with mortar and made fast under the roof slates. We tugged, pushed, pulled and swore some and it seemed as if the *plumbum* was winning the contest when suddenly the length of lead guttering gave up the fight and came suddenly free causing the four of us to fall unceremoniously on our arses in the rain gutter.

Knocker was first onto his feet and he said, 'Well we've got it, now what we gonna do with it.'

'Go an' get yer van, Knocker an' bring it round de back,' said Jimmy Mac, 'an' we'll frow this piece ont't coal pile, den we'll take it to Silverman's scrap yard on Travis Street near the Ancoat's Depot.'

The twisted sheet of lead was thrown over the parapet and we watched it fall four floors to the ground. It landed with a dull WHUMP on the coal pile sending up a cloud of dust. We all ducked beneath the parapet, where we held our breath for silence. We then exhaled slowly and rose to peep sheepishly over the edge, as if anyone seeing this massive airborne sheet of lead plummeting to Earth would not have known from whence it came. There was nobody about. With that Knocker scrambled down the fire escape and went to get his van. By the time he returned, Mitch, Jimmy and I had liberated and tossed a second length of lead off the roof.

We returned to ground level and with some difficulty manhandled the lead off the coal pile and into the back of the van. Jimmy and Mitch clambered into the rear of the vehicle; the tail board was raised and secured. I was working as Knocker's Van lad that day because Jake was on leave and Knocker was covering his round so I climbed into the passenger seat. While all this was going on, no one in the mess room had heard or seen a thing, thanks to the begrimed and opaque windows and the general clamour within.

In his haste to depart the yard Knocker drove, at speed, past the inspector's office and through the depot gates on to Great Bridgewater Street and almost ran into a passing police car. The Bobby inside the car slammed on as did Knocker and a collision was avoided by inches. The copper left his vehicle and came to remonstrate with Norman. We held our combined breath in case he looked into the back of the van where sat Jimmy and Mitch and about three hundredweights of stolen lead.

The officer approached the driver's side of the vehicle, removing from his pocket, his notebook and pen. He proceeded to give Knocker a severe bollocking and told him to drive more carefully in future and then, to our surprise, he glanced at his watch, put away his notebook and pen and said 'You're lucky this time.' He then turned on his heels, returned to his car and sped off. We had been let off, it seemed, because of a prior engagement or perhaps the officer was just late for his dinner. The near collision and the rebuke by the policeman happened within sight of the inspector's office, but Lady Luck must have been with us that day, as the inspector must have been elsewhere at the time. With much relief we watched the police officer depart. We then continued our trip to Travis Street and our clandestine dealing with the scrap metal merchant.

The scrapman, upon seeing four dirty and blackened young men looking somewhat shifty, seemed to realise that the metal for sale was of a suspect nature. He said, 'Throw it on the scales, lads and let's see what we've got?' He then tapped the side of his nose two or three times with the index finger of his right hand and told us, 'Be sure, I'll give you a fair price.'

In fact he offered approximately half the metal's worth and we were in no position to argue. It seemed that Lady Luck had now departed. Knocker asked, 'If we bring more can we strike a better deal?'

'Maybe, but we'll see how much you bring next time. O.K?'

'O.K. said knocker, see you soon.'

With that we returned to the depot and shared out our ill gotten gains.

This stunt was pulled one more time before misfortune befell us in the shape of a massive, electrical, rainstorm. The scrap metal merchant had raised his price on the promise of more stolen goodies but alas there was to be no more. A week or so later, after that torrential summer downpour, workmen were to be seen at the rear of the mess room hoisting sheets of lead and burning gear to the roof. The best part of two days was taken to reinstate the slates and put right the damage we had caused to the roof and guttering. Apparently a lot of damage had occurred within the offices below the roof space with a lot of secretarial equipment being ruined and damaged, not to mention the damage to such fixtures as carpets, light fittings etc. There must have been some hefty insurance claims registered at that time.

More roofing and ceiling contractors plus office fitters were there for the rest of the week. The perpetrators were never caught for that foolish misdemeanour, even though the police had been called in and had interviewed a mess room full of workers. They came to the conclusion that the offence had been planned and carried out by thieves in the night. Funnily enough the four amateur plunderers never ventured back to the roof for further ill gotten gains.

FREE SHOW

It's funny how new acquaintances are made and friendships struck, funny peculiar that is not funny ha, ha. Knocker and I became friends by virtue of the fact that we were both van lads of Jake and we shared a love of rock 'n' roll music. Joe O'Heeney and I became pals because he had already become a mate of Knockers through an interest in motor cycles. Jimmy Mac because he like me was a Blackley lad and a big Elvis fan. Mitch just happened to cotton on to us. Clarkie because of his mutual interest in motorcycles and because we breakfasted at Aston's Café most mornings. Dusty Rhodes was an old school friend who also joined the railways at Deansgate and became part of a fairly select group.

There were van lads that joined the railways later such as Dave Maybury, another motorcyclist. Also, there were the Onigbanjo brothers, Stuart and Jimmy, who were of African descent and of whom Jimmy was the eldest. There were also others on the periphery that joined the elite on their escapades.

There would be different permutations of this group who would go out together whenever the mood took them. On some Friday nights, directly after work we would go to the Haymarket or the St Matthews Tavern, two pubs on Tonman Street at the top end of Deansgate around the corner from what used to be the Youth Employment Office. Some of us were, legally, still to young to drink alcohol but in our work gear those of us that were too young passed muster. After a couple of pints the group would start to break up with some going home, some to finish their late shift and others going down to the Crown near Victoria to finish the night off or to meet their girl friends etc.

One Friday night, me, Knocker, Mitch and Dave Maybury and a couple of hangers on decided to venture onto Regent Road in Salford for the evening. We were all dressed pretty much the same, i.e. black leather jackets, blue denim jeans with the requisite contrasting turn ups. For whatever reason, the local guys in the Salford pub seemed to take exception to us, considering us to be interlopers from Manchester. Whether they thought that we were there to steal their womenfolk or not, I hadn't any idea, but the reason we were there was just to sample a drink in a different venue.

As the night progressed, looks were exchanged, comments were passed and really it would have been a good idea to vacate the premises somewhat earlier than we did. We were vastly outnumbered and so discretion being the better part of valour we decided to make our exit just before closing time. We left, only to be followed by a gang of youths whose intention it was to kick seven types of shite out of us visiting Mancunians.

The fight started shortly after we were subjected to a load of verbal abuse and some well aimed missiles. The police were called. The noise from the opposing factions coupled with the foul language and the sound of breaking glass brought an audience from the council flats opposite the pub. Balconies were full of cheering aficionados of the week end, pub brawl.

Two paddy wagons arrived within minutes, from the Crescent Police Station, from out of which tumbled a number of burly Bobbies. We felt a wave of relief; unfortunately we were wrong to do so. These law enforcement officers waded in, seemingly singling out us Manchester lads, like bloodhounds on the scent. They handled us roughly before handcuffing us and throwing us in the back of one of the vans. That night the only arrestees were railway employees from the Manchester area.

On the way to the Crescent Police Station the driver of the police van drove it around corners at speed and then immediately slammed the anchors on to make our excursion to the nick as uncomfortable as possible. We fell off the seats onto the floor and tumbled and bounced off one another, when one of the occupants, I don't know who but very probably Mitch, said 'Fuckin 'ell mate, yer can't drive!'

'Can't drive hey?' came the response, 'Well there's one thing I can do and that's fight and I'm going to show you just how well when I get you into the station. O.K?'

Then that voice again, 'Right, yer on.'

The van pulled into the Crescent's parking area, away from the roadway and any prying eyes and the rear doors were unlocked. It was my misfortune to be sat closest to the doors as they were opened and so be the first 'hoodlum' pulled out. A shovel like hand grabbed my jacket and heaved. Before I hit the ground, upon which I soon lay prostrate, I was hit a number of times by a fifteen inch length of varnished lignum vitae, commonly known as a truncheon. Having my hands cuffed behind me I could not raise my arms to fend off the blow, not that that made any difference as I believe blows would have been rained upon me until the desired affect was achieved. The pain was agonizing and blood poured down my face and onto my white T shirt. My battered being was then lifted and dragged bodily through the station, uncuffed and after the removal of my belt and shoe laces I was slung into a cell. I found out later that the other five arrestees shared two cells and were only slightly manhandled. It seems that I was considered the ring leader.

Through the night I asked, numerous times, if I could go to the local hospital. I was refused until the next morning when we were released from our cells and taken to the charge room where our fingerprints were taken and we were charged with public affray and thrown on to the streets to make our own way home or in my case to the hospital. My scalp was cleaned and stitched and the dried blood cleaned from my face. The nurse in attendance asked, 'How did these injuries occur?'

'The coppers beat me with a truncheon.' I replied.

'Don't be such a liar,' she said, 'our policemen; those protectors of the public, our dedicated and devoted defenders of law and order, those resisters of revolt and rebellion would never stoop so low as to use common violence, even against a lowly thug such as yourself.'

So much for that then.

In the next week's local Salford paper we were first page news under the headline 'Free Show at Free for All!' in which it reported that 'Balconies were like front row theatre seats when a gang of hooligans from the Manchester area taunted the local citizenry and fought like the ruffians they are. Windows were smashed and weapons used. One of the band of these marauding Mancunian youths had to attend hospital after being hit on the head by a flying bottle and Salford will be a quieter place after the arrest of these young thugs.'

To the Salford gutter press we were considered guilty before we had stood trial. About a month later we all received summonses to attend the Salford Courts, at Bexley Square, where we were all found guilty and fined £5.00 each. It was the first offence for each of us except Mitch who had been in court twice before. He had been arrested for stealing his own father's motorcycle in an attempt to elope with his girlfriend Pat who later became his wife.

It was the second charge that had us all gasping in amazement. It was read out in court that two years previous Mitch had been charged with the offence of indecent exposure. The rest of us, the accused, looked at each other in amazement, all sorts of thoughts went through our minds such as him waving his wand in a wanton way, flashing old ladies or young girls or anyone in between, but it transpired that he had been on his way home with his girlfriend when, after one too many espresso's in the coffee bar, his bladder, close to bursting, caused in him the need to urinate. He went behind someone's garage to relieve himself and was spotted by the owner of the property, who promptly phoned the police, resulting in his arrest and the indecency charge.

EARLY DRIVING EXPERIENCES

Sometimes, when time allowed, Jake would put me through my paces behind the wheel of the Scammell Scarab, to prepare me for the time when I would go to the driving school. These lessons would take place at the top end of the yard behind the Great Northern Railway Warehouse. He would have me practising gear changes, which was not easy for me as I had never driven before, let alone been in control of a commercial, articulated vehicle with a constant mesh, gate change, gearbox situated to the right of the driver.

At first I missed gears regularly and rattled the cogs so much in that gearbox that I thought I was in danger of destroying the transmission. Fortunately they are built to withstand the severe thrashing handed out by an amateur, gear crunching youth. Jake said that he thought that the crunching, grating and grinding was quite melodious and that he recognised one or two of the melodies that I'd attempted to play through the gear box.

Once I had, more or less, mastered going forwards and was somewhere near competent at gear changing, Jake suggested that I should learn to reverse the vehicle.

The Scammell Scarab only pulled a short trailer of sixteen to eighteen feet and because of this lack of length it becomes more difficult to reverse. This is because the transfer of movement from steering wheel to the articulating point, at the coupling, happens very quickly and the slightest movement or variation on the steering mechanism moves the trailer at a sharper angle than anticipated. The longer the vehicle the easier it is to reverse, odd though this may seem.

Most people know the theory of reversing an articulated vehicle and that the opposite lock to the direction one wants the trailer to go must be applied. Unfortunately it is not quite that simple in practise. One has to know when to put the lock on and when to take it off to avoid oversteer or understeer.

My first attempts at reversing were doomed to failure, I had that little artic tied in knots and Jake doubled up in laughter. I sent the trailer in the totally opposite direction to that which was required and at one time, when my foot slipped off the brake and onto the accelerator, I almost rammed the unit into the front off side corner of the trailer as the rig jack-knifed. Jake almost gave up on me, but luckily for me he persevered. Jake wasn't a bad teacher. I was a poor pupil, but slowly it all came together.

Other youngsters on the railway weren't as lucky as me insomuch as their drivers did not prepare them for the driving school. This, of course, did not deter some of the lads from training themselves in the evenings after the inspectors had gone home. Some youths drove just because they shouldn't and for the sheer hell and fun of it and this, of course, could easily lead to disaster.

One evening a 16 year old called Freddie Fox and his friend John Barber came across a Karrier Bantam with the keys in the ignition. The Karrier Bantam, which had a four speed, synchromesh gearbox, was hooked up to an empty trailer and the youths climbed into it. Freddie took the drivers position and John got into the passenger side. Young Freddie started the motor, engaged second gear; released the hand brake and let the clutch in as he applied some revs.

The vehicle started moving and as it gathered a little speed Freddie managed to change up to top gear. He drove past the mess room, from where I and one or two others watched. He then turned left, the engine groaning its reluctance as he cornered in top gear. He drove down towards the inspector's office and exit gate, gathering more speed on the slight decline as he went. When he reached the corner by the Inspector's office he again turned left, still in top gear and laboured the engine as he chugged up the straight towards the GNR warehouse, gathering momentum as he went. As he approached the warehouse he again attempted to turn left without changing down. At this precise moment, probably due to the undue strain it had been put under, the prop shaft snapped and dropped to the floor. It then caught between the cobbles and dug in. The cab rose in the air on the prop and because the vehicle was cornering, it started to roll to the right. After the cab had passed the apex the whole rig toppled on its right hand side amid a fireworks display of sparks, dust and smoke. It slid on its side for about twenty feet, spilling diesel and shedding body panels before coming to an unceremonious halt. The dust settled and then the passenger door was flung up and over. John Barber's head appeared from the cab, He was whimpering as he scrambled out and down to the cobbles.

Porters and clerks came running from the loading dock, startled into action by the overturning truck crashing onto its side and the subsequent noise from it sliding across the granite setts. They ran past the sobbing character of Barber to the truck to administer any help they could. From inside the truck, cursing and yelling could be heard. One of the porters climbed onto the cab and as he lowered his head to peer inside, he met Freddie coming up. Freddie Fox had started to extricate himself from the capsized truck and there was a clash of heads and Fox was heard to shout, 'Bloody Hell! Don't you think I'm in enough pain without you stickin' the fuckin' nut on me?'

'Sorry mate,' said the porter 'Let's get you out of there.'

Luckily, bar for a few cuts and bruises, neither of the young, unlicensed, wannabe drivers was hurt. The night staff from the work shop were summoned to recover the truck and trailer combination, which was a write off, and causing quite an obstruction. Both of the offenders had lost all hope of going to the railways driving school in fact they had lost all hope of continuing their careers on the railway. Both were called to see the inspector in charge and were given severe warnings and asked if they had anything to say in their defence. Neither of them showed any remorse or contrition for the events of the evening and so they were summarily dismissed. Still, after this unfortunate accident, self tuition by a number of van lads, continued unabated.

[2]A FIGHT IN THE MESS ROOM

On Friday afternoons, after the wages had been paid, various card games were undertaken in earnest and some individuals, especially callow youngsters, went away after having lost all their wages, having to borrow their bus fare to get home. It was on one of these Friday's, not long after I had been taken on, that a fight broke out between Clarkie and a black porter who was two years older than Clarkie.

The altercation was over a game of cards, three card, blind brag, if my memory serves me well. Clarkie and The porter, whose name was Yates, were the only two players left after the others that were in this game had folded and stacked their hands. The porter, Yates, ran out of cash and wanted to cover the kitty. Clarkie told him that if he didn't have the money he should not have joined the game and that he was claiming the kitty. The black youth jumped to his feet, knocking the table over and scattering the kitty and cards all over the floor.

He threw a punch at Clarkie who blocked it and went forward headbutting Yates but only catching him on the forehead. Yates grabbed hold of Clarkie and they grappled and wrestled for a few seconds when Kevin broke away.

There was biting, gouging, kicking and shoving; Kevin Clarke had the upper hand when Yates pulled out, from a sheath attached to his trouser belt, a Bone handled knife with a six inch

2. An alternative account of this incident can be found in the earlier book 'This Truckin' Life.'

blade. The fight was allowed to progress as long as there were no weapons being used but with the appearance of the knife a couple of the older drivers wrestled Yates to the floor. The knife was sent skidding across the stone floor and slid amongst the spectators where it mysteriously disappeared. It was actually picked up and secreted away by a drivers mate called Eddie Hunston, just in case the police were called. Inspector Etchells, as it happened, dealt with the matter within the confines of the depot. The two gladiators were issued with severe reprimands and were told that the slightest transgression in the future would finalise their railway careers. They were made to shake hands and promises were undertaken not to cause any more trouble.

These two fighters, whose faces had bumps and swellings and the odd cut, shook hands and made the requisite vows to cause no more trouble. The promises were almost broken soon after due to the unfortunate and foolish remark of a driver. Kevin Clarke's eyes were noticeably swollen and discoloured with contusions. The tactless driver of little sense shouted to Geddes Yates, who was similarly battered, 'You'll be alright Yatesy. Who's gonna notice a black eye or a fat lip on you?' Yates's second bout of the day almost started at this point as he leapt forwards in an attempt to take on the mouthy driver, but he was held back by the guys that had held him down when the knife appeared.

The kitty, which had been strewn about the mess room floor, appeared to have disappeared. it seemed that nimble fingered, fast on their feet van lads saw to its misappropriation and redistribution. It turned out that Clarkie had held in his hand three three's and Yates had a running flush. Thus Clarkie held the highest prial or three of a kind and so would have won the hand anyway. The fight was needless although very entertaining and Yates and Clarke held a grudging respect for one another after that.

The following week, old Tom, who at seventy years of age, came in at 0500hrs and had been kept on as a part time cleaner and to set the pot bellied stoves in the mess room and the inspector's office, was raking the ashes from one of the stoves in the mess when a blackened, pointed, steel implement came to light. It was obviously a knife blade. Tom picked it up, rotated it between his fingers, held it up to give it closer scrutiny and then discarded it with the ashes and clinkers into the rubbish bins, never to be seen again.

CHAPTER 4
THE OLD TIMERS

When I started at Deansgate there were a lot of older drivers, on delivery rounds, that were coming close to retirement age. Those drivers had known no other career than the railways. They were born just before or at the turn of the 20th century and they had left school just prior to or at the advent of the 1st World War and embarked upon a career which would terminate around 1963-1966. They were too young to fight in the 1st slaughter of the innocents and held on to their jobs under the protected industry status of the railway's industries for the duration of the 2nd Great War.

They were the generation that saw massive changes, such as the movement from gas to electricity for street and household lighting. They were amongst the first to use the disposable blade safety razor which was invented in 1895 and patented in 1901 by King Camp Gillette, Production started in 1903 and the device finally found acceptance after World War One.

In 1901 Daimler's Mercedes, the first viable motor car, took to the road followed, not long after, by powered flight at Kitty Hawk, North Carolina by Orville and Wilbur Wright (1903). In 1904 Courtaulds produced an artificial silk which later became known as Rayon.

Those older drivers saw the first movies and talkies and were amongst the first to witness electric vacuum cleaners (1901) and other electric powered domestic aids, which were invented prior to WW1. In 1906, an electric powered washing machine, designed by Alva Fisher appeared on the market and in that same year Reginald Fessenden made the first radio broadcast; a Christmas greeting to ships off the coast of Massachusetts. 1907 was the year Frenchman Paul Cornu achieved the first manned take off in a helicopter. 1909 saw the advent of the first commercial plastic, Bakelite, invented by Leo Baekeland. The first Diesel locomotive appeared in 1912, built by Sulzer of Switzerland. The invention of the brassiere in (1914) was a blessing for the well endowed female.

During the Great War in 1917, British and Canadian troops captured Passchendale in Belgium where half a million allied and German soldiers were killed. Also in 1917 GeorgeV proclaimed that his male descendants would bear the name Windsor. Plus in 1917 the Russian Revolution took place. In the US in that year 3 great jazz legends were born, Vocalist Ella Fitzgerald, pianist Thelonius Monk and trumpeter Dizzy Gillespie.

Ernest Rutherford observed the first nuclear reaction in 1919. In 1926 John Logie Baird demonstrated Television and in 1928 Alexander Fleming discovered the first wonder drug, Penicillin. In 1934 cat's eyes were invented by Percy Shaw, while in 1935 parking meters were introduced in America and in 1937 Frank whittle tested the jet engine and Nestle introduced instant coffee.

The Manhattan Project set up in 1942 after the attack at Pearl Harbour and to beat Germany to the production of an Atom bomb, resulted in the destruction of Nagasaki and Hiroshima which ended the Japanese involvement in WWII and was instrumental in ending the conflict.

In 1943 Jacques Cousteau collaborated in the invention of the Aqualung and the British mathematician Alan Turing's *Colossus* was proclaimed as the first computer; it was used to crack enemy, wartime codes.

After the war in 1945 Lazlo Biro's ballpoint pen was unleashed upon an unsuspecting public, then in 1946 the first two piece swimsuit, the bikini was launched followed in 1947 by the Polaroid camera. The De Havilland Comet 1, the first jet airliner took to the air in 1949. In the USA in 1951, colour television became available; it did not arrive in Britain until 1967. Non-stick frying pans came along in 1954 and a year later mass inoculation of Jonas Salk's polio vaccination turned the tide against this widely feared disease. Also in 1955 The Americans were the first to produce a nuclear powered submarine *USS NAUTILUS.*

The first giant radio telescope was built at Jodrell Bank in 1957. In the same year Boris Pasternak's Doctor Zhivago was published and Leonard Bernstein's musical West Side Story loosely based on Shakespeare's Romeo and Juliet took Broadway by storm.

Christopher Cockerell invented the Hovercraft in1959, and in 1961 Soviet Pilot, Yuri Gagarin became the first man in space but not before the oral contraceptive pill went on sale in the USA in 1960.

Launched in 1962 Telstar was the first active communications satellite. Its launch inspired a number one hit record for the Tornado's. In 1965 Mary Quant created the mini skirt.

This list of inventions, creations and changes that those older men lived through are only a fraction of those that occurred and the time will probably never be beaten or even equalled as an era of social and economic change.

Those elder statesmen of the railways had also seen the transition from horse drawn delivery vehicles to delivery vehicles powered by the internal combustion engine. The first of these being the Scammell Mechanical Horse and although this was originally introduced in 1932 it was not until the late 1950's that horses were phased out completely.

The drivers that once drove the horse drawn vans simply transferred their skills from horse to powered vehicle without having to take a further test. In those days of yore, when traffic density was nothing like we have to contend with today and vehicles had a lot less power it is excusable that this was allowed to happen. The horse drawn vehicle was, after all, articulated with the front axle and shafts being attached to a turn table.

After working for fifty plus years for the railways those older drivers retired with a nice watch and a meagre pension. So small was the pension in those days that the old timers applied, as did Old Tom, to stay on after retirement, to do the menial job of lighting the pot bellied stoves and cleaning up to supplement their incomes, but there were only so many jobs on the railways. Some of the drivers such as Teddy Taylor applied for a job, at sixty five years of age, with C&A Department Stores working with their in house security. Yet others struggled along, trying to make ends meet as best they could.

Life expectancy was not as long those few years ago and those ex railwaymen could only look forwards to working till they expired or to a retirement spent in poverty. Gladly things have changed for the better, although the manual worker, in general, will never experience a life of luxury or the longevity of the more affluent within society.

CHAPTER 5
A LITTLE ABOUT OTHER DRIVERS AT DEANSGATE AND THEIR ESCAPADES

At the time I started at Deansgate there were drivers of all ages from those that had recently passed their tests to those about to retire. These drivers from Deansgate covered the Southern and Eastern parts of Manchester. The Northern and Western parts of the town and parts of Salford were attended to by drivers from Victoria Parcels Depot.

To remember all of the drivers at Deansgate, at that time would be too much of a feat of memory but some that come to mind are: Albert de toper who was good friend of Jakes. That friendship, I believe, stemmed from the fact that they were both motor cyclists. Jake had ridden a 600cc, Norton Dominator 99 with the famous featherbed frame. I don't recall what Albert rode but it was said he once owned a 1,000cc Vincent, Black Shadow.

At one time he had had a rather nasty accident. In this accident, which happened before I started at Deansgate, Albert, it seems, lost control of his machine and rode it into a ditch. When he finally came to an abrupt halt the clutch lever penetrated his left hand and came out the other side. When Albert was taken to hospital the knuckles of the hand had to be removed leaving Albert with a deformed appendage, south of his wrist. After his convalescence and on his return to the work place he was told he would have to take another driving test, as it was deemed his injury may stop him driving safely and correctly, after all this was the hand used for gear changing and applying the handbrake on most vehicles. Albert passed the test with flying colours and he later went on to drive 32 tonners at Freightliner.

Albert's round took in the parts of Hulme that Jake's did not plus part of Moss Side and Brookes bar and Old Trafford. On this round were two breweries, Hyde's and Swales' plus Pomona Docks at Cornbrook, where the Guinness boats dropped off their loads from Ireland. Albert, who liked a drink, took advantage of this and visited the breweries and Guinness, on a daily basis, to obtain his allowance, whether he had anything to deliver or not. Being well known on his round he took his allowance at all three outlets. The result of this was a rather rubescant flush, extending from his nose outwards to his cheeks which always had an unhealthy floridity with the occasional outbreak of pustules.

One morning, when Albert was on his way to work, he passed a certain house and saw a flickering light inside and smoke creeping under the door. He forced his way into the property and led the residents from serious injury or death. A neighbour awoken by Albert's forced entry into the property phoned the emergency services.

Albert received a commendation for his public spiritedness and because his rubicund complexion was mistaken for burn marks he was awarded a payment from the public purse for his bravery and the injuries that he had sustained.

William (Bill) Bailey was what one would describe as a 'much disliked, niggardly and miserly, miserable sonofabitch.' He made his van lad of the day sit on the back of the truck whatever the weather. On no account would he let his lad ride in the cab with him. He never treated his lad to a meal as did all the other drivers; come to think of it he never treated himself to a meal, he was too stingy to pay canteen prices and so brought sandwiches which he ate in his cab whilst his van lad sat miserably in the back of the van.

Bailey elevated parsimony to an art form. He would accompany the lad on every delivery, making sure the nipper toted what ever was to be delivered. The reason he accompanied the youngster was in case a gratuity was proffered. If so it would be immediately snatched by Bailey and pocketed, the lad never saw anything of the tips that were given. Quite at odds with the way Jake treated me. I was allowed to keep all gratuities except at Christmas when tips were shared equally. All the other drivers shared or gave all the tips to their lads. Bailey was the Fagin of Deansgate, working his lads hard and taking all the profits.

On his round was Lewis's Department Store and at times and out of sight of the security man, Bailey could be found rummaging in the bins at the rear of the store for oddments or things that were broken but could be repaired or weighed in or sold on for a profit. Despite his free travel passes Bailey told those that wished to know why he delved into waste bins that the money he made on these salvage operations was enough for two continental holidays a year.

Whenever Bailey was seen approaching by a bunch of van lads they would start singing 'Bill Bailey won't you please go home.'

Knocker worked as Bailey's Van lad for his first year on the railways and had nothing but contempt for the man. He eventually escaped the clutches of Bailey and went working with Jake prior to me. On his first outing with Jake, Knocker went to the rear of the vehicle and clambered into the back, thinking that that was the norm after working with Bailey. Jake went to the rear of the trailer and asked 'What are you doing up there? You're not with Bailey now, come on, get in the cab.' And so Knocker found out what it was like to work with a decent driver.

John (Chalkie) White was a middle aged driver whose round covered the university areas of the South side of Manchester along Wilmslow Road and all student accommodation areas off campus around Platt Fields, Victoria Park, Rusholme and surrounding areas. There was nothing spectacular about Chalkie; he was just a very nice person who minded his own business and worked hard delivering shipping trunks to student accommodation and various mail order parcels to domestic properties. His was a very busy round. Chalkie owned a very nice Ford Consul 375 which he later sold to Knocker.

There was Albert Shaw, another good mate of Jakes, although he was a couple of years older than Jake. Albert had one of the busiest domestic rounds in the depot, delivering around a section of Wythenshawe, which at the time was the biggest council estate in Europe. Albert's deliveries were almost all mail order from GUS, Marshall Ward's or any of the other big mail order houses. Albert was a big man physically with a sense of humour to match.

Because the Wythenshawe rounds were mainly domestic, mail order deliveries and because there was very few afternoon collections these drivers on the Wythenshawe rounds went out with around a hundred deliveries and worked all day solely to disburden themselves of all the mail order packages.

Norbert (Nobby) George, another friend of Jakes, delivered to the Heald Green area and other parts of Wythenshawe that Albert Shaw and others didn't. His was also a big and busy round, which contained a few industrial premises such as Sharston Industrial estate and around Roundthorn. Nobby transferred later to Trafford Park Freightliner Terminal as a Class one driver.

There was another driver on the Wythenshawe rounds by the name of Billy McMahon. I think Billy's round covered the more industrialised areas of Wythenshawe around Timpson Road where there were a number of factories and warehouses. He delivered and collected at Timpson's Shoes, Nicholls' Vimto factory, and a whole host of others plus household deliveries of mail order goods.

Phil Wetherhilt was yet another mate of Jakes and around the same age. To me, at the time, Phil looked like the type of person you wouldn't like to meet in a dark alley at night. He appeared to be hewn out of granite with a countenance that was positively frightening. In actuality he was an easy going, quiet spoken individual, so don't be fooled by first impressions. Phil was the fourth and final driver on the Wythenshawe area.

Bob Hoey was another roundsman. I cannot remember whereabouts he delivered or who his van lad was but Bob was an average type of guy who caused nobody any bother. He, like Jake, was on the LDC, (Local District Council), which was appended to the NUR, (National Union of Railwaymen) and undertook to resolve any local grievances.

The drivers that worked the Wythenshawe area were amongst those that joined Jake and me at Aston's café for breakfast, although they stayed much later at the café than me and Jake. There was, of course, an ulterior motive to this. These men would return to Deansgate depot at approximately 1900hrs thus guaranteeing their overtime without having to do a trip to the Knightsbridge bakery, which entailed hard, manual labour.

There were two brothers Albert and John Worsley, both approaching middle age with Albert being the elder. Both were roundsmen although I cannot remember which round either covered. Albert was a rather introverted chap where as John was a total extrovert with boundless energy and could be best described as young at heart. I seem to remember that both the Worsley's were active within the union.

The rounds in the city centre were mainly undertaken by the older drivers who had moved on to easier rounds as their seniority allowed. Manchester was all open in those days. There were no pedestrianised areas, no Arndale Centre. The Old Shambles was in its original spot, old pubs like the Fatted Calf were still around. Withy Grove still had its hen market and the Smithfield fruit and vegetable market was still on Shude Hill, with the fish market adjoined. The vehicles used on these city centre rounds were small urban delivery, rigid, four wheeled vehicles and these delivery rounds were deemed the best to be on at the time.

Teddy Taylor did the Piccadilly and Market Street round, taking in most of the big stores of the day such as Paulden's, C&A, and Woolworth's, etc; he had graduated from horse drawn vehicle to a motor without having taken a test.

On the same type of round was another oldster who had gotten his driving license by way of grandfather rights after working on horse drawn vehicles as a carter. His name was John (Jolly) Carter. Carter by name carter by profession.

Dave Lee, who left the railway in the mid 1960's, to take up employment at Ringway Airport, (now Manchester International Airport), also had a town round. Dave had a military bearing, walking with shoulders back, chest out. He didn't so much walk as march. He had been on the railway for years, his railway service only interrupted by his National Service, so it came as a surprise to all his workmates when he handed in his notice, but I suppose, to some, the grass is always greener on the other side.

There was Old Harold, the driver whose brew can had become detached from its handle. He too had a town round. Harold was fast approaching retirement age and was a relatively new man to the railway and so he just kept his head down and got on with his job.

A younger man that held a town round was a black gentleman by the name of Frank Fitz-Herbert Bailey. Fitz, as he was known, went on to work at the Trafford Park Freightliner Terminal. Why his town round was never claimed by one of the older drivers, by way of seniority, I don't know.

There were other drivers, younger of course, that were on shift work. Seniority worked in a way that becoming a roundsman meant stepping into dead men's shoes. One didn't get the job unless someone died or retired and then that job was thrown open and the most senior man that applied got the job and so on until the job that was left was the one nobody wanted. That was the opportunity for a shift man to break the yolk of unsocial hours, to do a day job he didn't really want until the next retirement or death came along and the free for all bidding would start again. Some drivers cherished their town rounds other drivers wouldn't take a town round under any circumstances.

Of the shift drivers there was Gerry Mahoney, an overweight, myopic driver of about twenty one years of age. He lived in Blackley not far from me. For a Railway's Road Vehicle driver he would have made a very good demolition derby driver; he had more bumps, prangs and scrapes than any other dozen drivers put together. Eventually he was made to undergo another test which he passed. This surprised most of the other drivers because they didn't believe he should have passed his test the first time around. His accident rate, however, did go down.

Walter Wall, a cousin of mine, started on the railways, at Deansgate about a year before me. Walt already had a full license and had started at Deansgate as a driver but he had to pass the railway's domestic test for each vehicle he drove. Every driver had to take these domestic tests to prove his confidence and ability to drive each type of vehicle at the depot.

Walter was into any money making scheme he could find. He used to take orders from the workforce for meat, be it lamb, pork or beef. He would then use whichever railway vehicle he had been allocated for the day and go down to the abattoir to pick up the freshly slaughtered meat. He had already purchased weighing scales and a meat cleaver and he would set up his own little butchers shop at the top end of the loading dock where he would cut the meat into the requisite sizes and he would become 'Walter Wall, Purveyor of fresh Meats.' He bought the meat at wholesale prices and sold it below retail, making a nice little profit. He was helped in this endeavour by Johnny Worsley.

Walter lived in Blackley Village where his brother in law owned a garage virtually opposite Walt's little terraced house. When Walter had time, usually around dinner time, the railway vehicle that he was employed to drive could be found parked at the garage and Walt would be inside rubbing down body panels of cars that had been in for repair, earning yet more undeclared income.

Walter had a reason for all his scams, of which there were many. His ambition was to save enough to buy a pub in the Isle of Man and move over there lock, stock and barrel. By the time he was twenty three he had realised his ambitions and is still in the Isle of Man. Walter's only failing was that he could not get out of bed in the early morning. When I moved onto shifts at age eighteen, Walter would give me a lift to work on the occasions that we were on the same shift. On early shift I frequently had to wake him by throwing stones at the bedroom window after his alarms had failed to waken him. Morning birdsong, which readily woke me, had no effect on Walter's sleep patterns. It would have taken the Gigantic Roc of Arabian mythology to awaken Walter. He eventually went onto a regular night shift to avoid getting up early. This, of course, gave him more time to find other clandestine jobs to earn the money to fill the coffers to fund the pub.

Whilst on nights Walter had a rather strange experience on his return trip from the newspaper run to Chester. As he passed a well known picnic area, which was in a lay-by off the A556 around the Winsford area, a young woman, wearing very little and that which she wore was in a state of dishevelment and disrepair, ran into the roadway screaming and waving her arms frantically in a gesture for Walt to stop. As Walter pulled up, a car sped out of the lay-by with no lights on and disappeared into the night. The young lady, her lip bleeding and mascara running down her face was crying hysterically as she flung herself into the passenger side of Walt's vehicle.

'He- he-he tried to r-r-rape me! She stuttered through her sobs.

'Hold on there,' Said Walt as he put his railway great coat around her shoulders to spare her any further indignity. 'Button it up or you'll catch your death and then tell me what's happened.'

The somewhat bruised, young lady explained, between sobs, how she had foolishly accepted a lift home from a nightclub from a stranger. This person had then attempted to have his way with her sexually in the picnic area. The young lady had put up a fight and had finally broken away from her assailant. She managed to open the door of the car and then she made a run for it in the scantily dressed mode in which she encountered Walter.

Walter listened patiently to the young lady and offered her his handkerchief and a hot drink from his flask. He then drove her to the nearest police station where she was looked after and Walt was detained for about three hours being interviewed, telling his version of events and making out statement. Whether or not the alleged, would be rapist was ever apprehended I don't know but I don't remember Walt ever attending court as a witness to this event.

Clive Thorney was a West Indian Immigrant who was determined to fit in. So much so that he adopted a white mans hairstyle, putting a parting in his hair and pulling his tight curls straight, with the effect that he was going prematurely bald. Clive was a dedicated idler. He was so workshy that when he was hospitalised with a hernia, another driver was heard to say, 'Thorney must have got that hernia farting, 'cos that's the only time he ever strains hisself.'

Clive was vanity personified and had neatly manicured hands and fussed over his appearance like a lady. He was a fop, a dandy and also a dedicated womaniser. He believed himself to be the answer to any and every maiden's prayer.

Roy Woolstonecroft who was maybe two years younger than Jake was a tall slim guy. He was, I remember, an easy going guy. Roy was a confirmed bachelor who only showed aggression when playing football, at which he excelled. He never wore his uniform trousers but preferred denims which he wore unwashed until a new pair was required. Sometime, a few years later, his resistance to wedlock was gradually broken down by a lady of perseverance who finally became his wife.

Games of football were played at dinner time on the cobbles and tarmac of the yard. There were very few rules to the railway's version of soccer although a lot of skill was shown by the better players. The players had to run, dribble, shoot and score goals whilst dodging and weaving between the iron support stanchions within the depot.

It was obvious and inevitable that accidents would and did happen. One such accident happened to Ronnie Bennett, one of the clerks, who after a somewhat robust, retaliatory tackle by Jake Barlow, was sent reeling towards the four foot where he momentarily stopped and teetered on the brink. He swayed one way and then the other in an attempt to maintain his equilibrium before he finally lost his balance and fell over the edge where he landed awkwardly between the disused tracks, twisting his right ankle, which was left pointing outwards at an impossible angle.

He was helped up from the track and supported, as he hopped, carefully to the rear of the loading bay and placed gently at the foot of the steps. Ernie Etchells was summoned to witness that place where the clerk lay, moaning in agony and where he had supposedly had his accident. The injured party was taken to the Manchester Royal Infirmary where more than one fracture was confirmed. The accident was registered in the accident book as a tumble down the loading dock steps and so Ronnie was able to claim an industrial accident. He was away from work for three months.

Players regularly fell over the four foot and onto the disused railway lines but injuries were mainly of a not too serious nature such as scrapes, cuts and bruises and sprains with the occasional dislocation and fracture when footballers were pushed into or collided with the support stanchions. Tarmac gravel and cobble rash were the main types of injury, caused when players went or were brought down and the knees or hips of their trousers were taken out on the rough surface being played upon. Clothing was regularly torn by opposing players fouling the player in possession, sleeves were pulled away from jackets and/or waistcoats, shirts were victims of aggressive play with buttons flying, like bullets, every which way, but all in all it was an enjoyable pastime, relished by all who played.

Mike Shannon, a porter at Deansgate was an Irish lad of twenty one years who had come back from the railway's driving school at the end of my second week at Deansgate. He had passed his test in a Scammell Scarab but soon had his domestic license filled with all the other various vehicles. He was a good driver but his ambition was to drive buses for Salford Council. Within a year he left and took up employment at Weaste Bus Depot in Salford.

An offshoot of this is that a couple of years later when my girlfriend and I were saving to get married, my girl became a clippie at Weaste Bus Station so as to boost our savings. Her driver turned out to be Mike Shannon.

Joe O'Heeney was a newly passed out driver when I started. He became a close friend of both Knocker and me. Joe was of Irish descent and hailed from the Moss Side and later Hulme districts of Manchester. He later transferred to the Freightliner Terminal at Trafford Park. Joe is about a year or two older than me.

Joe lost an eye in an industrial accident, whilst at Freightliner, and was medically retired at sixty years of age. The accident happened as he was in the process of opening a container of which the custom handles were very stiff. Joe stood on the rear under-run bar of the trailer and pulled on the handle as hard as he could when, without warning it unexpectedly sprang free. The suddenness with which this happened took Joe completely unawares and with the handle being at head height it struck him in the eye. Joe lost the sight in the eye although the actual orb was saved. Cosmetically, I suppose, that was better than having to wear a glass eye.

Roger Cronshaw or Big Rog transferred into Deansgate from Bury. Roger was a giant of a man with a barrel chest. He was also known as the Bear. Roger was, literally, a big Elvis fan and wore his hair in the Presley style sporting a high pompadour and long black sideburns. Rog was a Blackley lad and lived just around the corner from me; indeed I had known Rog since I was nine years old although he was four years my senior.

It was one of Roger's van lads that was responsible for releasing a twenty stone pig onto a passenger platform at Piccadilly. Roger and his nipper had attended at Piccadilly livestock office to collect the said boar. It was on a pull along truck, incarcerated in a stout wooden box, which did not allow for much movement within its confines. The lad, whether by accident or purposely, undid the catch that secured the door on this portable pig pen. The porker, sensing freedom, pushed its way through the door and jumped to the platform and started running around like a pig possessed, causing people to flee in terror until it was cornered in an empty guards van of a local train. From there it was enticed back into its cage and sent on its way. The van lad, a youth of known mischief, pleaded accidental escape on the pig's behalf and nothing more was said or done about the incident.

Big Rog had a whirlwind romance with one of the girls from Kightsbridge Bakery. He married the girl and they went to live with Roger's mother, unfortunately the marriage only lasted a couple of days before they separated. The lady wife had had an argument with Roger's mother and Roger had leapt to his mother's defence. This was too much for the newly married Mrs Cronshaw, who had expected loyalty, devotion and support from her new husband and she immediately packed her belongings and left. Marry in haste.......etc.

Mr Cronshaw was a gentle, giant of a man and he doted on his elderly mother and a few years later whilst he was working at Freightliner, his mother, after a lengthy illness, passed away. At this time Roger and his mum were living in a high rise block of flats in Haughton Green, Denton. His mother's death affected Roger badly and he drank more heavily.

One of his ambitions was to watch a football match at every league ground in Great Britain and shortly after his mother's death he went to Glasgow to watch the derby match. Roger had taken a few drinks before entering the ground and once inside he got into an altercation with a couple of Glaswegians. This erstwhile gentle, giant of a man was still grieving and he seemingly lost the plot. Although he had never hit anyone before or raised his hand in anger, he walloped the two Scotties, knocking them both out and it took half a dozen policemen to escort him from the ground. He spent the rest of the weekend in the cells and was weighed off in the sheriff's court, via a fine, on the Monday morning, thus he missed a days work at Freightliner back in Manchester.

Sadly Roger died in an accident at home a few years ago. He had been out drinking and when he returned home he took a tumble indoors striking his head. This blow proved fatal. He is missed by all who knew him.

With Roger, from Bury, came another Blackley man, Terry Griffiths who lived in the same avenue as Roger. His nickname, spoken in a Bury accent, was 'Turry from Burry. Terry was a middle aged driver who had worked on the railway from being a lad, and he used his seniority when he came to Deansgate and soon had a delivery round. He was a pot bellied; flat capped jovial man who would sing at the slightest opportunity. He actually earned a few bob singing in the local pubs around Blackley, Harpurhey and Collyhurst and he had a fine baritone voice.

Yet another driver who hailed from Blackley was Fred Wright. Fred was an unambitious, slow talking, slow moving individual, He was about four years my senior. He left the railways' when Deansgate closed.

From the Langley area of Middleton came two Drivers that were very close friends; they were John Lord and Tony Crème. John Lord was actually a son of Blackley who moved too Langley after he married. Tony was a weight lifter cum body builder who liked to be called Tony Reeves after Steve Reeves the American Mr Universe who played Hercules in the film of the same name. In actuality Tony was a mere shadow of Steve Reeves. Both left the railway before the closure of Deansgate.

Dick Christopher was a West Indian Immigrant. He was a bit of a bluff character and seemed to think the world owed him a living.

Another West Indian immigrant was Vinny Powell. Vinny was just the opposite of Dick, he was an easy going, droll character who forever had a smile upon his face. Vinny was responsible for turning over a partly laden Scammell Scarab and trailer. That incident happened as he tried to beat a set of traffic lights on his way to Mayfield Station. He attempted to corner too fast and ended up with the vehicle leaning at approximately forty five degrees against a lamppost. When help arrived Vinny's van lad was stood by the vehicle pretending to strum a banjo and giving a very credible version of George Formby's '*I'm Leaning on a Lamppost at the Corner of the Street in Case a Certain Little Lady Come's by,*' to applause from passer's by. Vinny stayed in the cab sat behind the wheel in an attempt to appear less visible; for once the smile was missing from his usually beaming face.

George Pembo, another of our commonwealth cousins, came to Great Britain in the late 1940's with his parents and siblings. George became a good friend of Jake's and later of mine. In his spare time he played in a Caribbean steel band. Much later George transferred to Lynx Logistics and was made redundant at sixty years of age. He got quite a lump sum as his service from the railway carried over to Lynx. He hadn't been out of work for more than a couple of hours when the management at Lynx realised that they had let too many men go. George was offered his old job back and was allowed to keep all his redundancy.

He went back a much richer man than before he was made redundant. George retired in 2007.

There were two drivers on shifts that bore the same name. Both were called Gerry Gaskell. The elder of the two was a rather laconic, lugubrious, pipe smoking individual aged at the time in his mid thirty's. Like most people of his age he had served in the armed forces via conscription. Although he was an overweight, lumbering individual, nicknamed 'Plod', he was once offered outside by Clarkie, once again over a game of cards. Plod slowly stood up, shrugged his shoulders in resignation and followed Clarkie outside, closing the door behind him. About thirty seconds later the mess room door opened and in walked Plod. Me, Knocker and Mitch dashed outside to see Clarkie sprawled out on the floor. He was just coming round so we helped him up and took him inside to recover. He and Plod, once outside, had squared up to each other; Kevin Clarke had rushed Plod who swung a right hook which landed flush on Clarkie's temple. Kevin's knees buckled and he went down; out cold. The moral of this is, 'Don't mess with the older guys, they may have more experience.'

The other Gerry Gaskell was a resident of Moss Side; he was a slim, bespectacled, quiet sort of fellow who also ended up driving at Freightliner, Trafford Park. He had the unusual hobby of collecting pocket watches and wore a different one on each shift, he kept much to himself.

I remember an occurrence that happened whilst Gerry was still at Deansgate. He was doing the same night run as Walter Wall was doing on the night Walter had picked up the distressed, half naked lady. Gerry had tipped his load of newspapers at Chester and was empty and on his return journey to Manchester. He was proceeding along the A56 and decided at approximately 0500hrs that he deserved a brew.

He parked up on the A56 near the village of Helsby adjacent to the BICC cable works. After brewing himself a mug of tea, using his Thermos Flask for that purpose, he settled down, in the passenger seat with his brew and his copy of Playboy, for a well earned break.

It was pitch black at that time of the morning when Gerry noticed a pair of headlight beams top the hill a couple of hundred yards in front of him. As he watched the vehicle draw closer, the thought ran through his head that the vehicle approaching him seemed to veer onto the wrong side of the road and was heading straight for his motor. At first he thought it was a hallucination, a weird play between dark and light. He was very soon to find out differently.

The other vehicle, a petrol tanker, was travelling at excessive speed and before Gerry could do anything the glaring headlights filled his cab with a brilliant, blinding light which left Gerry temporarily blinded. There then came the terrible impact and the railway's vehicle was shunted backwards under the force of the bigger and heavier truck. Gerry was thrown around the cab like a rag doll. Then........ Silence, everything was quiet, Gerry had lost consciousness.

Upon regaining his awareness and gathering his senses he managed to scramble from the mangled vehicle. The pain he felt was almost unbearable; he experienced aches and pains over every part of his being and one of his wrists was limp, swollen and obviously fractured.

Both of the vehicles involved in the incident were so badly damaged that they were both later written off. The railway vehicle was one of the recently acquired walk thru vans, probably a Bedford or Commer 7 Tons GVW; and the violence of the smash had crushed the bonnet and pushed the engine into the driver's compartment. The steering column and the driver's seat were twisted out of shape and had been pushed through the bulkhead into the cargo compartment. Gerry Gaskell was a very lucky man indeed to have survived such a crash. Fortuitously he had decided to use the passenger seat to take his break because he would have had more room to stretch out and rest in comfort without being hindered by the steering wheel and column which may very well have crushed him in the aftermath of the collision.

After the accident someone of unknown identity, upon hearing the noise of the collision, had telephoned the emergency services who arrived within minutes of Gerry returning to the land of wakefulness. The police, ambulance service and fire tenders all arrived within seconds of each other. The driver of the tanker had to be cut free from his vehicle and both he and Gerry were ferried to the local hospital.

Gerry, of course, who had been parked quite legitimately, on the correct side of the carriageway, with his side lights illuminated at the time of the pile up, was cleared of any wrongdoing and the tanker driver was charged and convicted of dangerous driving.

Luckily the driver of the tanker had discharged his load and was returning empty to his depot at the Stanlow oil refinery.

The tanker driver, in a statement to the police and in mitigation, explained that some object had fallen from the dashboard to the floor and he had tried to retrieve it. That was when he had lost control of his vehicle and careered into the railway vehicle. It was the general consensus, of all that knew of the accident, that the driver of the tanker had fallen asleep at the wheel.

Other drivers that I recall by name only at Deansgate are Bill Cooper who worked the Gorton area, Kevin Pulford, and John Coller. Coller had a brother who was an engine driver at Piccadilly. There was Mick Taylor who was the recipient of the flying brew can mentioned earlier. There was also a guy from Macclesfield, a tall, thin, middle aged, bespectacled man, whose name I can't recall who had a tendency to ride the clutch and thus burn that element of the transmission out on any wagon he drove. I think he transferred to Macclesfield Station as a porter out of embarrassment. He just couldn't keep his left foot of the clutch pedal.

As there were two drivers named Gerry Gaskell, there was also a second Frank Bailey who unlike Fitz was a white man. He also was a roundsman that ended up as a class one driver at Freightliner. There were other drivers at Deansgate that came and went and yet others that I cannot remember, so those mentioned do not comprise a comprehensive list.

CHAPTER 6
GOODS & PARCELS DEPOTS AROUND CENTRAL MANCHESTER

DEANSGATE PARCELS DEPOT

Deansgate Passenger Parcels Depot was located at the junction of Great Bridgewater Street and Watson Street and was housed beneath and adjacent to the lines that ran into Manchester Central Station and behind the Great Northern Railway Warehouse. No trains ran into Deansgate Parcels Depot during the period that I was employed there.

The workforce that was employed at Deansgate when I started there was originally employed at Manchester London Road. The horses that were used whilst at London Road were stabled in Store Street and what motorised vehicles they had were garaged at North Western Street, which was also the workshop. The move to Deansgate was necessitated by the increase in Passenger Parcels Traffic and because of the refurbishment of London Road Station, which after the face lift would become Piccadilly Station.

Deansgate ceased to function around about the same time as Victoria goods depot with staff retiring or accepting redundancy or transferring to Freightliner or Oldham Road Goods Depot.

MAYFIELD

Mayfield Station opened in 1911 as an overspill station for Manchester London Road (now Piccadilly). It was closed to passengers in 1952. Mayfield was situated adjacent to London Road and it was the terminus for many suburban lines. As Piccadilly is once again running out of capacity there has been a proposal to re-open Mayfield Station as either a block end station as it was before, or to extend the lines through the station to join the existing line to Oxford Road, or even as a dedicated line to Manchester Airport.

Mayfield was gutted by fire in mid 2005. The station is also said to have its own ghost which has been heard since the 1980's. It is said to take the form of ghostly footsteps echoing in the building late at night and is thought to be the footsteps of a suicide, of which there were a number around the mid 20th century.

Mayfield was re-opened for a short period in 1970, as a parcels depot employing a lot of ex Deansgate, Victoria and Oldham Road staff. Since its closure Mayfield has been used as a location for television productions. The most notable of these was as a den for drug traffickers in Granada's Prime Suspect, starring Helen Mirren and as the 'The Sheffield Train Station' in the drama, The Last Train.

LIVERPOOL ROAD GOODS STATION

The building of Liverpool Road Station started in 1830 as a passenger station. Shortly after, goods offices were constructed adjacent to the passenger station. Soon after opening it was realised that both passenger and goods traffic were exceeding expectations and it was evident that additional facilities were needed. The station was extended along Liverpool Road with shops on the ground floor and a canopied carriage shed above.

The shops were not a commercial success and were later used as workshops and office space. There was a lower yard to Liverpool Road which was accessed from Water Street. Two new warehouses were built in 1831 for the storage of cotton, and at the same time a transit shed was built for speedy transhipment of goods from rail wagons to horse drawn carts.

All passenger traffic ceased when, in 1844 all passenger trains were re-routed to the terminus at Hunt's Bank Station (now Victoria Station), which was seen as a more convenient location for the rail network expansion. Liverpool Road then became solely a goods station, operated by the L&NWR from 1846. Around 1855 the transit shed was demolished in favour of a longer single storey facility. There was a major conflagration, in 1866, whereby one of the storage warehouses was all but destroyed and the other badly damaged. Both had to be demolished.

In 1869 The Grape Street Bonded Goods Warehouse, staffed by HRH Customs, was built and in 1880 a large warehouse was built with a frontage on Lower Byrom Street. This was the last major addition and Liverpool Road Station remained much the same for the next 100 years.

British Rail finally closed Liverpool Road in 1975 and part of The Museum of Science and Industry opened on the site in 1983. City Hall adjacent to the station accommodates the rest of the museum.

It was on the opening of the Liverpool to Manchester line in 1830 when a number of trains were coming from Liverpool to Manchester, Liverpool Road Station that the first railway fatality occurred. William Huskisson, 1770 – 1830, MP for Liverpool and supporter of railways was invited along with various other notables including The Duke of Wellington, Robert Peel and a Dr Brandreth and Surgeon Hensman to travel in the cavalcade. Huskisson was riding in The Northumbrian and when the trains stopped at Parkside, Newton Le Willows to take on water he crossed from his carriage to visit and to converse with The Duke of Wellington. As he was stood on the track warnings were shouted that Stephenson's Rocket was about to pass the Northumbrian. Huskisson attempted to board the Duke's carriage but The Rocket Struck him, badly mangling his leg. The doctor and the surgeon applied a tourniquet to stem the bleeding and the MP was lifted onto the low bedded bandsman's carriage of the Northumbrian and George Stephenson used this train to take him for further assistance, but Huskisson died later that day.

VICTORIA GOODS STATION

Victoria Station is the second of Manchester's main line stations and is also a Metrolink Station. Originally it was a small single storey, single platform building designed by George Stephenson. The station was enlarged by William Dawes and in 1909 boasted seventeen platforms.

The goods station was linked to the passenger station via a water powered hoist in Hunt's Bank, (The Stations Original Name), off Victoria Street where the entrance to the goods depots lower yard was to be found. The upper yard of the goods depot was off New Bridge Street, opposite Boddingtons Brewery. The goods depot ceased to exist sometime in the 1970's and the land is now occupied by the Manchester Evening News Arena and car parks.

Adjacent to Victoria was Manchester Exchange Station which shared a platform with Victoria. This Platform, at the time, was the longest in Europe. Both Victoria and Exchange were served by the LMS. Exchange Station had a goods and livestock office. The entrance and approach to Exchange Station was off Victoria Street and there was an exit down the Salford approach to Blackfriars Road.

MANCHESTER CENTRAL STATION

In the 1870's the GNR, The Midland's Railway and the Manchester, Sheffield and Lincolnshire Railways had no station facilities of their own in Central Manchester. They amalgamated to form the Cheshire Lines Committee (CLC).

The engineer for the newly formed CLC was Lewis Henry Moorsom who was chosen to build the station and work was commenced in 1875.Central Station had a massive single span arch constructed by Andrew Handyside & Co. This arch is 210 feet wide, 550 feet long and at its highest point stands 90 feet and at the time of construction was recognised as an exceptional piece of engineering. The arch spanned six platforms and nine tracks.

Manchester Central Station opened in 1880 as a passenger station, but as a certain amount of goods, including livestock were carried on passenger trains, Central Station had its own parcels and livestock office. The station closed to both passengers and goods in May 1969. The operating company at the stations closure was the LM Region.

The station building is still standing and has been converted into the G-Mex exhibition Hall and conference centre which opened its doors to the public in 1986. The railways property and arches adjacent to G-Mex are now mainly used as car parking space.

OLDHAM ROAD GOODS & PARCELS DEPOT

Oldham road opened up in 1841 as the terminal for The Manchester & Leeds Railways. The goods section of this railway yard was originally known as Thompson Street Goods Depot. When the line was moved into the newly opened Victoria Station

Oldham Road became solely a goods depot. Companies such as Rowntree's chocolate and Fyffe's Bananas had their own unloading docks at Oldham Road. It functioned until the late 1970's when it closed and staff moved to a section of Mayfield Station for a few years. On the site of what was Oldham Road Depot now stands The Royal Mail sorting office, a Chinese Supermarket and a fire station.

ARDWICK WEST GOODS YARD

Ardwick West was accessed from Devonshire Street down Blind Lane; an old cobble stone Road that ran under the railway arches that carried the lines that ran into Ardwick passenger station and Piccadilly Station. The goods yard was situated behind the GUS office building which is now used for other enterprises. Ardwick West carried bulk cargo alongside A and B type containers which were the forerunners of the ISO type containers. The operating company at its closure was the LNER.

ARDWICK EAST GOODS YARD

Ardwick East Goods Depot was situated and accessed off Ashton Old Road on the same line that fed Ardwick West and carried much the same traffic. The lines into Ardwick East were block end spurs from the main Piccadilly to Stockport line; the spurs were just after Ardwick junction coming from Piccadilly. This goods yard was also operated by the LNER.

ANCOATS GOODS STATION

Ancoats Goods Station was situated behind Piccadilly Station on Adair Street adjacent to the old St Andrew's Church site. It had a superb subsidised canteen. The land where the depot stood has been converted to various small industrial units and the Royal Mail Parcel Force Depot. The area is a well known red light district.

The rail line which crossed the Medlock to Ancoats Goods Yard is long since demolished.

All of these goods yards and stations are within a mile of Piccadilly Station with some virtually within a stone's throw. Piccadilly Station besides having a Livestock and parcels office had its own goods depot next door to the passenger station on Ducie Street, into which goods trains ran. Sadly like the rest it has disappeared.

CHAPTER 7
A TRAILER BOY ON SHIFTS

EXPLODING VANS, DEAD CATS & RUMOURED DEATH IN THE ANTIPODES

Jake and I worked together until the week of my eighteenth birthday. I was allowed to finish the week off on days and report for duty at 0530hrs on the following Monday. The advice I received from Jake was to apply for the driving school before I went on to shifts. Following Jake's advice I put forward my application and hoped it would soon come my turn to learn to drive commercial vehicles professionally.

My driver on my first week on shifts was to be Knocker and I met him walking through Albert Square at 0515hrs on the Monday morning. He was in front of me but I recognised him from the rear by his finger tip length, black, drape jacket with padded shoulders. He wore drainpipe trousers terminating at his ankles thus displaying his brightly coloured socks. On his feet he wore size nine's, thick crepe soled, wedged heel, brothel creepers. From the rear in the misty morning fuzziness he resembled a child's blackboard and easel that had, by some magical means, learned the art of perambulation. Knocker was one of the last of the Edwardian styled Teddy boys with his big quiff, long sideburns and Edwardian garb. I caught up with him and we walked the rest of the distance to the depot together.

.

When we reached the depot and had clocked on Knocker was allocated his vehicle for the day which was a diesel powered Dennis. We then went to the mess room to enjoy a brew before work commenced. While Knocker made his log sheet out I went and checked the vehicle over. I found it low on fuel and told Knocker so. After consuming our cups of tea we proceeded to the railway's fuelling point on Baring Street below and to the rear of Mayfield Station.

Once fuelled up we were to collect a load from Piccadilly for Deansgate. We proceeded to Piccadilly and as we approached and slowed down at the security box at the top of the station approach there was an unexpected, deafening bang and the engine cover inside the cab blew off and shot up in the air to hit the ceiling of the vehicle and fall back with a resounding thud, in a skewed position. The cab was then immediately filled with thick, black, oily smoke.

Knocker, unable to see, due to the acrid, smoggy atmosphere in the cab, tried to steer to the kerb side, but because of the diminished view he drove onto the platform beyond the security box, where he managed to bring the vehicle to a rest. He then scrabbled for the door handle, in order to bail out of the cab, in an attempt to reach safety. I, thinking only of self preservation, had actually exited the cab and hit the tarmac before the vehicle had been brought to a complete halt, unsure whether our lives were in danger or of what had caused the explosion.

Scrambling along the tarmac, closely followed by Knocker, who had stumbled around to the passenger side of the vehicle we made for the security box amid clouds of the same black, oily, noxious miasma that had filled the cab. We staggered and reeled to the rear of the vehicle, towards where the security box was situated. Tears were streaming from our eyes and our mouths and nostrils were filled with the pungent thick vapour causing us to retch and cough. Our faces were covered in the greasy, sooty residues from the smoke.

Stumbling and falling, we bumped into the security officer and a couple of porters who were standing well back and staring inquisitively at our unusual, smutty appearance The oily, black residues had been spread all over our faces as we attempted to wipe away the lachrymal flow from our stinging, red rimmed eyes. One of the porters said that we resembled a couple of Al Jolson impersonators on a bad day.

The security man pointed out to Knocker that he was, in his temporary blinded state, helping to keep death off the road by driving on the platform. That, as we found out later, was not the case, however, because as Knocker drove up on to the walkway one of Piccadilly's oldest, feral felines was sat there grooming itself. As the goods vehicle approached amid the thick cloud of its own making, the cat stopped its toilet, its body arched and stiffened and it became rooted to the spot with fear as it seemed to watch, mesmerised, as the vehicle got closer.

The marmalade mouser was wide eyed and frozen in terror until the last second when it made its futile bid to escape, alas it was too late. The vehicle hit the poor moggy; there followed a shrill feline shriek and the pussy cat was crushed to death beneath the off side front wheel of the vehicle which is where it lay lifeless as Norman and myself vacated the vehicle. The cat's wail as it died was unheard by us as we attempted to extricate ourselves from the stricken vehicle; we had other things on our minds at the time.

The cloud that surrounded the vehicle soon dissipated and realising that we were not in any imminent danger we calmed down. The air became clear again and Knocker climbed back into the cab and refitted the engine cover as best he could. He then released the handbrake and engaged reverse gear and turned the ignition key. The vehicle would not fire, but on every turn of the ignition key it struggled backwards until the vehicle was back on the roadway and off the body of the cat, which lay prostrate and crushed, with blood around its eyes, ears and mouth, its carcase flattened like the cartoon cat from a Tom and Jerry film. One of the porters who were present went to fetch a shovel and that poor, old, deceased grimalkin was roughly shovelled up and thrown, unceremoniously, into the waste skip to be taken to the tip; that was its final send off for several years of loyal and dedicated employment keeping down the rodent population at the station.

All the goods stations and indeed Passenger stations had resident mousers of the genus *felidae*. Some passenger stations had two or more cats whereas most of the goods and parcels depots usually had only one cat. The sole purpose of the railway cat was the persecution and destruction of the rat and mouse population that were forever present in the depots and stations.

The problem with the exploding vehicle, it appears, was that Knocker unknowingly and unwittingly had put petrol in the diesel powered motor which had run for a while and then under pressure and heat the petrol had exploded blowing the engine cover off and scaring us half to death. I hate to think of the consequences had the explosion occurred whilst progressing along a main road.

The roughly treated vehicle was towed away, for remedial work, to the railway's workshop, which was situated in the railway arches on North Western Street, below the lines into Mayfield Station. Knocker and I were ferried back to Deansgate in the next available vehicle.

Once back at Deansgate we cleaned ourselves up and then Knocker had to explain what had happened and fill in a defect report for the vehicle. He was sent to Hunt's Bank, to see the head man, a Mr Ricketts, to be told how stupid he was and how his irresponsible action had cost the company a lot of money to put right and that if it happened again he might face the sack. As it happened Knocker received a written disciplinary warning, which is a fairly severe disciplinary measure.

The rest of the week Knocker and I were on what was commonly known as the broccoli run. The job was a 0530 start and entailed loading up at Piccadilly or Mayfield with deliveries of fruit, vegetables and flowers for Smithfield Market on Shudehill. Because of the narrowness of the cobbled roadways within the market, Scammell Scarabs and trailers were the driver's preference for this job with the Karrier Bantam and trailer running a close second. Of course any type of vehicle would be used if the favourites were unavailable. Indeed private hauliers delivered to the market with top weight artics.

After we had delivered our first trailer load we would pull up outside the market café on Swan Street where we would meet other railway drivers that were on the early shift and go in for our breakfast. That café opened at 0400hrs to cater for the marketmen and from that time onwards served dinners of meat, potatoes and two veg or fish chips and peas or Burgers etc; that was because, at the time we went into the café and earlier, some of the market men already had four or five hours under their belts and that was their dinner time. Knocker and I plus the other railway staff joined those marketmen in their repast. I had not realised just how good fish, chips and peas could taste at 0630hrs in the morning.

Having done our second trailer load to the market we would then finish the day executing trailer changeovers at the GUS warehouse in Ardwick, whose loading bays were at the junction of Devonshire Street and Higher Ardwick. The GUS warehouse would have up to four drivers working all day taking empty trailers or trailers of returned goods and returning to Deansgate, Victoria, Mayfield etc; with loaded trailers, where the parcels would be sorted for destinations further afield. If any more drivers were required at GUS daymen would do a load for overtime.

Not everything that happened at the Deansgate depot had a happy ending; in fact there was the occasional sad occurrence. There was an episode concerning two brothers that had started work as van lads on the week I went on shifts. Their surname was Rowlands and they were very close in age. The elder brother was called Frank and the younger brother's name was Barry. When they started they related to anyone who cared to listen, how in a few month's time they were emigrating from England to Australia, with their mother, to start a new life. They were going on the £10 Assisted Passage, (They would be known as £10 Poms), that scheme ran from 1945 until 1972 and was taken advantage of by millions of Brits at the time.

The time came for the Rowlands' to depart and depart they did. Within a very short time, however, rumours abounded that they had perished, so it was said, in a train crash. Of course this tragedy, if it did occur, happened thousands of miles away in the antipodes and not actually at Deansgate. Still, it caused people to think and register concern and a certain amount of irony, considering the railway connection, for the family who had given up everything to start a new life in a new and faraway land on the other side of the world.

Working as a trailer boy/van lad on shifts one did not have a regular driver and theoretically a van lad could be with a different driver every day of the week. Usually a lad was teamed up with a driver for a full week and often longer. I, at one time or another, during my short time as a mate on shifts worked with most of the shift drivers, sometimes perhaps, for a hour only on an overtime run. All the shift drivers were decent men and most of the lads got on well with them. That was because we had worked with some of them when they themselves were trailer boys and we were closer in age to them than we were with the roundsmen.

The accident rate was higher amongst the younger drivers. That was prompted mainly by the impetuosity of youth coupled with a devil may care attitude plus the fact that the period after the driving test was the time that the young, hot headed, and sometimes impatient drivers actually started to learn what driving professionally was all about. Most of the accidents suffered by the younger drivers were no more than slight prangs resulting in a few scratches. The incidence of rear end collisions was higher in the course of the younger driver's days, but as the learning curve shortened these incidences became less prevalent as professionalism overtook youthful exuberance and irresponsibility.

KNIGHTSBRIDGE CAKE

It was after going onto shift work, or turns as shifts were called on the railway, that I was first sent to Knightsbridge Bakery on Ayres Road in Old Trafford. On the way to Knightsbridge Cakes was a very good and competitively priced alternative to the railway canteens. That alternative was called Val's café on Skerton Road and it was sited opposite the Mother's Pride Bakery. Val's was a regular port of call for Railway road vehicle drivers on route to or from Knightsbridge. At any time of the working day there would have been from one up to half a dozen railway's liveried vehicles found parked on Skerton Road outside the café.

There were usually a few railway vehicles, from both Victoria and Deansgate, waiting to be loaded as well as vehicles from privately owned haulage companies. Four loading bays were to be found at the front of the building and one to the rear of the building where the loading was affected through a narrow, shuttered hole in the wall, through which were passed lengths of extension rollers to slide the cartons of cake along.

The loading of cake at Knightsbridge was probably the most physical job that the Deansgate and Victoria staff had to do. Without a doubt it was backbreaking work with continual bending and straightening carrying and stacking large boxes of cake. When loading at the front bays, the cake was brought to the vehicle on pallets to be off loaded onto the vehicle. One of the railwaymen would climb into the rear of the vehicle and his mate would then unload each box of cake from the pallet and hurl it along the floor of the vehicle. The man in the back of the vehicle would then pick up and stack the boxes in layers until the required amount was loaded. Occasionally a roller would be placed on the floor of the vehicle to slide the boxes along. It was all handball and the procedure was re-enacted in reverse when unloading at the destination station.

At the rear the boxes of cake came to the vehicle via a chute to which was attached a roller and one of the team working the wagon would go inside the bakery to slide the boxes along the rollers to his mate who would be in the rear of the vehicle and whose job it would be to stack the boxes. The job was double the effort if the cake one was loading was Iced Genoa which was twice the weight of any other type of cake due to the layers of marzipan and icing sugar. The loading of iced Genoa was the cause of many lost days due to back strain and pulled muscles.

Often, a railway driver would let an unsuspecting private haulier go before him if it meant not reversing down to the hole in the wall. The only saving grace about loading at Knightsbridge was that every loader was given a large piece of cake, weighing approximately 2-3lb. There was no way I'd eat the cake, I'd seen how it was made, so I usually gave it away or sold it to the local corner shop near home.

It was on a return trip from Knightsbridge Cakes that the driver that I was working with was racing with another driver to see which one of them could reach Mayfield station and get off-loaded first. My driver tried, in vain, to overtake the other driver at the most inopportune moments; on blind bends and whilst approaching road junctions and traffic lights. There were one or two close encounters with other vehicles whereby evasive action had to be taken. There were times that I thought I was caught up in a Keystone Cops chase. I hung on to the door handle and seat, with white knuckles, anticipating the worst.

I was sat, during that race, in the passenger seat of a Scammell Scarab which my driver of the day drove with what can only be called complete and reckless abandon. The vehicle that my driver was trying to outdo was a six cylinder; petrol powered, Bedford which was, without any doubt, the fastest type of vehicle owned by the depot. It was being driven, somewhat rashly and unwisely, by a newly passed out driver who had every intention of winning the race.

Surprisingly, both vehicles made it to Mayfield without any major incident or without being stopped by the police and as my driver followed the Bedford through the gates at Mayfield and then took, at too fast a speed, the immediate left hand bend, the vehicle in which I was the passenger leaned dangerously to the off-side and the drive wheels on the near-side of the unit plus the near-side trailer wheels left the ground. It was only the fact that we were loaded with iced Genoa, which is a very heavy fruit cake with marzipan and icing that stopped the vehicle toppling over and into the brick wall to our right. The iced Genoa, because of its weight, took fewer boxes to make up a three ton load. That kept the centre of gravity fairly low and thus saved the vehicle, the driver and me from disaster.

My driver, upon recovering his composure after almost turning the vehicle over and realising that the race was lost, drove up the rest of the approach and onto the main thoroughfare of the station, which ran parallel to the platform of the station, at a more sedate pace. The sight that greeted us brought a smile to my driver's face as he pointed towards the far end of the platform. At the top of the station prior to the block end buffers, with its nose in the air and its rear end resting on the rail tracks, was the six cylinder, petrol powered Bedford.

The driver in his haste to win the race and not having realised that my driver had capitulated had driven down to the end of the station and pulled to his right. As he had stopped, his van lad had jumped out and ran to the rear of the vehicle to guide his driver as he attempted to make a three point turn. The driver pushed the clutch pedal down and slammed the gear stick into reverse and floored the accelerator which caused the vehicle to shoot backwards. Apparently he didn't hear his van lad shout WHOA!!!

The van lad leapt out of the way as the laden vehicle flew off the platform and over the four foot. At about half way down its length the underneath of the truck struck the edge of the drop with a flurry of sparks; severing brake lines and fuel lines. The back end hit the tracks and the truck stopped dead. The load, which had no restraints, slid backwards and made good its escape; tearing the roller shutter from its holdings and scattering three tons of fruit cake over the tracks.

The shutter hung down and flapped in the breeze, its broken slats lay with the cake on the tracks. The mangled tail board hung down at an angle and rested on the rail tracks and all was quiet; nobody moved, then, as if somebody had switched the power back on, numerous people dashed forth to render assistance to the stricken driver.

The signal box at Piccadilly had to be contacted and told to hold any incoming trains outside the station until the line was cleared. Salvage operations began a little later and the vehicle was pulled off the tracks and taken to North Western Street garage for repairs. As much of the cake that was still boxed and not crushed was stacked onto pull along trucks for sorting. The crushed boxes were thrown into the rubbish bins, which still left a lot of mangled cake on the track. Mayfield station had the best fed rats and sparrows in Manchester.

The driver, whose name escapes me, was paraded in front of Mister Ricketts, the head honcho at Hunt's Bank, by whom he was severely reprimanded and like knocker and many other drivers before him was threatened with the sack if there were any recurrences.

There was no doubt in my mind that a lot of the cake, that was still packaged and in good condition, found its way into the cabs of the various drivers that were present and into the cars of the porters at Mayfield to be eaten at dinner time, taken home or maybe sold.

SKIDS AND JACK KNIVES

On a wet autumn morning I reported for work at 0600hrs to be greeted by my driver Mr Gerry Mahoney. We were to do a run to Mayfield and return to Deansgate from whence we would work on trailer change-overs at the GUS Mail Order Company in Ardwick.

The usual vehicle checks were carried out by me. The unit that we were allocated was a three ton, Karrier Bantam, urban artic. After the vehicle had been checked and we had drunk our cups of pre-duty tea in the mess room, we returned to the vehicle which Gerry drove to his allocated trailer. He reversed the unit under the trailer, all lights were checked and the number plate affixed to the trailer and off we went with our loaded trailer to Mayfield.

The trip to Mayfield and the return to Deansgate with a full load for distribution amongst the delivery rounds was completed without any problems. Gerry dropped the trailer on one of the loading bays and drove around to the GUS returns bay where a full trailer of returned goods awaited us. He reversed under the trailer while I got out of the cab and released the trailer brake; he then pulled forward a few feet so that I could get behind the trailer to pull down and secure the shutter and fit the number plate. Having done that the lights were checked and we were ready to roll with the trailer packed full with returned mail order goods.

The outward journey to GUS was uneventful and upon reaching GUS the trailer of returns was dropped in the yard and our outgoing trailer was picked up and pulled out of the loading bay and dropped next to the incoming trailer. The inwards trailer was then picked up again and deposited in the then empty loading bay to be loaded later. The outward bound trailer was then picked up again. All connections were made, the trailer brake released, the number plate affixed and we were ready to deliver the trailer to Mayfield, a journey of less than one mile. A distance, one might think, in which nothing could go wrong….. WRONG!

The Bespectacled, myopic Mr Mahoney pulled off the GUS yard onto Devonshire Street, opposite Ardwick West goods yard, almost knocking a cyclist off his bike as he did so. He then turned down Temperance Street, which ran parallel with North Western Street, to join Fairfield Street close to the entrance to Mayfield. He drove towards the junction with Fairfield Street a little too hastily. It was raining that day and the roads were wet and slippery, as he neared the junction he applied the brakes. The brakes on the unit acted in accordance with their design and the drive wheels locked up slowing the unit down but causing the vehicle to skid. Unfortunately, it seemed, that the brakes on the trailer were not quite up to the required standard of maintenance and the trailer which, in reality, was travelling faster than the unit started to push the whole rig forwards and around.

The trailer was loaded to its full three ton capacity of mail order goods and being so much heavier than the prime mover it began to come around from the rear. I glanced through the corner window to see the rear of the trailer trying to overtake the cab, and then there was the inevitable impact, which took the form of a sickening, metal wrenching, crunch as the side of the trailer crashed into the unit on my side and began to push us further around. It turned a full three hundred and sixty degrees and then a further ninety degrees before colliding with a stationary car that was parked in the road. That collision brought the spinning rig to a sudden halt, causing it to almost topple over. The whole combination of trailer and tractor leaned over precariously to approximately thirty degrees from the vertical, stopped momentarily in the balance and then crashed back down leaving the jack-knifed vehicle straddling both lanes of the roadway.

Whilst I watched all of that happen through the rear and corner windows of the unit, it appeared to be taking place in slow motion. It was like a well choreographed ballet and just before the impact between trailer and cab Gerry was heard to yell 'Oh shit!' To which I responded 'Oh fuckin' 'ell!' before I was bounced out of my seat and thrown across the cab to land unceremoniously in Gerry's lap. The force of the trailer slamming into the cab shook Gerry's glasses from his face and they had flown out of the open window of the cab into the roadway.

When the Terpsichorean performance of the unit and trailer had reached its finale and I had managed to disencumber myself from my driver's knees, we both clambered from the stricken vehicle. The short sighted driver had his arms stretched out in front of him so as to feel his way. He resembled the short sighted, cartoon character, Mr Magoo, as he fumbled around without his glasses. I, in the meantime, surveyed the damage to the vehicle and trailer.

My driver, by then had gone down on all fours and was making sweeping motions, along the carriageway, with his hands as he tried to locate his spectacles. They were found a little later in the gutter with the arms twisted out of shape, lenses badly scratched and the nose piece broken but perhaps, temporarily, repairable.

The trailer was barely scratched but the near side of the unit was stove in. The rear and corner windows had been popped free from their seals. The corner window had been shattered into a million shards of toughened glass strewn along the highway, along with Gerry's broken specs. The rear window lay inside the cab unbroken. The stationary car, which turned out to be abandoned was now an abandoned, stationary, wreck, fit only for the scrap yard.

The North Western Street Road Vehicle Workshops were just around the corner and so I ran there to notify the garage staff of our little mishap. A mechanic was sent to the scene, in a Scammell Scarab, to render assistance. The damaged Karrier Bantam was released from the trailer and the Scammell put in its place and with a great deal of care and skill, by the mechanic and not by Gerry, I might add, the trailer was pulled away from the car. By that time the police, who just happened to be passing, as they do when you least need them, pulled up and statements were taken, and the wrecked car was reported and later towed away.

The mechanic drove the badly bent Karrier to the workshops followed by Gerry and me in the Scammell and trailer. The myopic driver had retrieved his spectacles from the gutter and he wore them in a lop-sided and twisted fashion.

At the workshop the brakes on the trailer were adjusted and tested and the rear axle checked for alignment. The trailer was given a visual inspection for further damage, and found to be OK to continue with the job, after which it was taken back to the workshop for further investigation.

Gerry wore the broken glasses, upon which he had affected a temporary repair by making good use of the workshop's medical box. The eyeglass frame had numerous revolutions of sticking plaster wound around it at the bridge of the nosepiece. They still sat in a lop-sided and twisted fashion upon Gerry's face and he may not have been able to see perfectly through the badly scratched lenses but, hopefully, he would by then have had slightly better sight than Mr Magoo, although that would have been a moot point. His spectacles were in a better state than they were before the temporary repair and so with me continuing to act in the capacity of his trailer boy we carried on with the job.

Luckily, after making out an accident report and following an investigation and not least because of the faulty brakes, Gerry was absolved of all blame for that particular incident. Mister Mahoney heard nothing more from the police and it is supposed that the wrecked car was scrapped. I took a few days sick leave to recover from the sprains and strains, bruises and pains that I had suffered that day, as did Gerry Mahoney.

NIGHT SHIFT

The night shift came around every third week and was usually from 2200hrs until 0630 but could be elongated to twelve hours either by pre-rostered overtime, which meant starting at 1830 hrs or, much more rarely, by adding on the hours after the rostered shift i.e. finishing at 1000hrs.

The purpose of the night shift at Deansgate and Victoria initially took the form of a clearing up job; clearing the remnants of the mountains of parcels that the late shift had left and that had come in as collections from the roundsmen.

When the clearing up operations were finished the night shifts duties were to deliver the first edition morning newspapers, in bulk, to major distributors or to do the first deliveries on the broccoli run to Smithfield Market or take any livestock to Piccadilly or any of the other main line stations. Some of the night shift's newspaper runs, such as the run to Chester, Preston and Carlisle, were small trunk runs to the newspaper distributors and were virtually long distance runs for the city depot.

TALES OF THE RAT AND THE HOOKER

My first stint on nights found me coupled with a driver by the name of Phil Landerer and we were working the bare shift of 2200- 0600 hrs; on the night in question we had done our first load of the shift and had returned to Deansgate at just later than midnight. Our next job was a newspaper run to Rochdale and for that we hadn't to be on Exchange Station platform until 0230. Phil said to me 'I didn't get much kip through the day so I'm gonna get my head down for a couple of hours. Give us a shake at two o' clock.' And with that he pulled one of the dining tables in front of the pot bellied stove, turned off the light in that section of the mess room and climbed onto the table and lay along its length supinely with his arms crossed on his chest resembling a corpse laid out for viewing. Within a couple of minutes he was snoring quietly and melodiously.

I sat in the other half of the mess room and tried to read a paper in the dismal and dim light of the nicotine stained, single, sixty watt lightbulb. At 0200 I went to awaken Phil. As I walked into the section where he slept I noticed a movement in the half-light. My eyes adjusted and became acclimatised to the gloom and I could make out a vague silhouette on my sleeping driver's chest, of a large rodent of the genus *Rattus-Rattus*. In the dim, flickering light cast by the dying embers of the stove it appeared bigger than it was. I stared, hypnotised by the sight of this buck toothed, coarse haired rodent which was sniffing Phil's face, its quivering snout almost touching the snoring man's lips.

The whiskers of that grey/brown beast tickling his skin must have awakened Phil. His eyes sprang open and he was greeted by the sight of a twitching, pointed nose, two, sharp, yellow incisors and two beady, gimlet eyes staring into his own from close quarters. He screamed. The rat squealed and bounded off his chest over his face and onto the floor; it scurried towards the closed door and squeezed itself underneath it through a gap that seemed impossible to allow an exit. Phil leapt up gibbering something unintelligible whilst brushing his chest and face with his hands. Unfortunately the rat had been as scared as he had been and it had left a very real and tangible deposit upon Phil's chest and the brushing only served to spread the rat's excrement about his person. Ironically the noise awoke the depot's big ginger she cat that had been sleeping blissfully, on a chair, in the other half of the mess room. It stretched, exposed its claws, yawned, looked around, rolled over and promptly went back to sleep.

It was all too much for me and laughter came unheeded, needless to say Phil had not seen the funny side of this episode. My laughter came so hard that I was doubled up and got a stitch and the hearty chuckling brought tears to my eyes but finally it subsided and I did my best to help Phil clean himself up in time to pick up the newspapers for Rochdale. Luckily, on that night, Phil was wearing a pullover over his shirt. He removed the badly ordure stained woollen garment and deposited it in the pot bellied stove, leaving him with a lesser fouled shirt, but I'm afraid the stench of rat pooh hung around Phil for the rest of the night.

Rat faeces and urine can transmit the bacteria leptospirosis ictero-haemorrhagiae in the form of Weil's disease. The illness that these bacteria may cause manifests itself as influenza like symptoms, jaundice and liver failure and has a death rate of approximately twenty five per cent; Phil and I were quite ignorant of this disease at the time and as they say ignorance is bliss.

Another driver I had the misfortune to do nights with was the accident prone Gerry Mahoney who, one night while I was working with him, picked up a prostitute near Piccadilly. Because of the lack of room within the cab the hooker sat on my knees whilst Gerry drove back to Deansgate.

She was what I considered to be the archetypal middle aged whore with face make up that appeared to have been applied with a trowel. The bright red lipstick that she wore went over and beyond the contours of her mouth and it seemed that she had bathed in gallons of cheap perfume. Her habiliments on that night were a short plastic raincoat, a short skirt and low cut blouse which was opened low enough to show off her wares, which were copious.

At the depot Mahoney sent me to see if there was anybody in the messroom. My report back to him was that there had only been one driver and his lad plus a couple of porters having their meals in the mess. A curse issued from the mouth of my driver and he told me to go and sit in the messroom for ½ an hour while he drove to a quiet part of the yard to get his money's worth from the whore.

I went to the messroom and I was immediately asked as to the whereabouts of my driver. I related to the others there where my driver was and what he was up to. They took this as a sign to have some fun at Gerry's and the working girl's expense and maybe to indulge in a little voyeurism. They stopped what they were doing and went out into the yard to locate the van cum knocking shop. They soon found the vehicle which was rocking with the actions of the copulating couple within and from which grunting and moaning could be heard.

The driver amongst those would be fun loving peeping Tom's got stealthily into the cab and within the short space of a few seconds; he had started the engine, put it in gear, accelerated forward a few feet and slammed on. There was an awful racket of tumbling bodies and grunting and moaning of a different kind from the back of the van. The porters and the van lad then dashed to the rear of the vehicle and pushed up the shutter. There on the floor of the van, thrown up against the bulkhead, legs entwined, but barely visible because of the lack of lighting, were Gerry and the trollop in various states of undress and dishevelment. Gerry had cursed and shouted 'You fuckin', lousy bastards!' as he disentangled himself and tried to put away his, by then, flaccid member. The hooker had cursed and shouted at Gerry 'You fuckin', cheap, lousy bastard!' as she tried to pull up her panties with one hand and hide her titties with the other, although it seemed rather strange to me that a prostitute would feign coyness and false modesty in such a prudish way. We didn't really see much in the shadowy darkness in the back of that vehicle but the occurrences of that night were talked about for weeks to come.

Once their attire was adjusted and the cursing and giggling had quietened down, Gerry had to drive the streetwalker back to her chosen place of operations. On the way back to Piccadilly, with the hooker sat on my knees once again, Gerry tried hard to negotiate a discount for *coitus interuptus* but the strumpet would have none of it and exacted her full fee and she had even demanded a little extra money for the inconvenience which, under duress, Gerry eventually paid.

The night shift drivers, as a matter of course and if time permitted would pick up their friends that were on the early shift, and deliver them in good time to the depot. Those that they could not pick up they would clock on. The van lad would also clock his mates on so very few people were ever shown to be late. There were, at the time, bus services which ran through the night, but then as now buses weren't that reliable. Even the early shift specials that were brought on to accommodate early shift workers were unreliable. It was much better to be picked up, especially during the winter months when the mornings would be cold, wet and miserable.

The night shift was a relatively comfortable shift; the work was easy because there was very little supervision. Upon starting the shift at 2200 one would find numerous clocking on cards stacked behind ones own. These belonged to the late shift workers that had gone home early and needed clocking off. It was seen as a duty to carry out that act even though it was completely beyond company policy and could result in the sack, although I never heard of anyone facing this ultimate punishment. The clocking in and out of ones workmates and other staff was endemic on the railways at the time and I believe that the inspectors and foremen knew it went on but turned a blind eye for the sake of a smooth running depot.

The night shift was a shift that was not to my liking. Sleeping through the daylight hours was the problem that I suffered and there were plenty of others like me. Fortunately there were just as many who loved the night shift because the pay was at time and a third with the opportunity to work twelve hours. Consequently those that didn't want night work swapped with those that did and everyone was happy and hence, people ended up doing regular night shift.

LATE SHIFT AND THE CROWN

The late shift drivers and lads, after 1730, had the job of running between Deansgate and Mayfield Station and Victoria/ Exchange Stations with supposedly full van loads. Those loads were the parcels that had been collected by the roundsmen and sorted for their destination stations. Of course there was a dodge that was used by the lazier partnerships of drivers and mates. If no supervisory staff was watching a wall of parcels would be built approximately half way down the vehicle and the load carrying space would be filled up from this wall, meaning that the vehicle was only half full. Unfair on the hardworking staff but the slackers and shirkers didn't care.

If the inspector on duty suspected a wall was built he would climb into the rear of the suspect vehicle and hurl himself at the load. If it collapsed towards the front of the vehicle and his suspicions were proven, he would make the culprits stack the load from the front, ensuring a full and fair load. Sometimes, of course, his suspicions may have been wrong and he would throw himself at a solid, unyielding stack of parcels and would then have to climb back down to floor level somewhat red faced and apologise for doubting the loaders integrity.

The inspectors on shifts were usually based at Victoria but would work at Mayfield on a rota basis. One of these inspectors went by the name of Clarrie Freeman. Clarrie was fair man that got on well with all the drivers but he would not stand for people taking the Mickey at work. Another of the shift working inspectors was Bill Parkinson.

Bill also got on with all the drivers; he was an easy going guy and did not like confrontation, Bill was a war veteran and drivers, over the years, had learnt that if Bill could be tempted into a conversation concerning the war, which was his favourite subject, all thoughts of work disappeared in his reverie and recollections and very little work was seen to take place.

On the late shift, loads were taken from Victoria to Mayfield and vice versa. Often when the vehicle had been emptied the drivers and their lads, from both Deansgate and Victoria, would frequent the Crown Inn which was situated virtually opposite Victoria's lower level yard. Drivers would park at the rear of the Crown so as to be out of sight of the depot and its inspectors.

At the time the Crown was run by a blonde divorcee who was getting on for thirty years of age. She was a good looking woman with a young son aged about four. She had a nice, full figure but she also had the reputation of being somewhat amoral and promiscuous. There was a driver at Victoria called Jimmy Coleman who had a reputation for womanising and at the time was going out with the blonde landlady. One Friday night whilst unloading at Victoria prior to going over to the Crown, Jimmy, me and Knocker, who I was working with that week, were talking when Knocker asked of Jim, 'Are you still knocking about with that bird from the pub?'

'Yeah,' said Jim 'I'm not givin' up a good shag like that, 'specially when there's no commitment.'

'Are you seeing her tonight?' I asked.

'Course I am,' he replied 'I'm workin' tomorrer mornin' so I'll shag 'er later and stay for the night then when I get up in the mornin' I've only got to cross the road and I'm at work. I hope she's put that bloody kid of 'er's to bed though.'

'Why's that?' I enquired.

'Well, t'other night I 'ad 'er upstairs; she was stark naked, on the carpet, in the front room. It was after closing time. Mi trousers were round mi ankles and I was shaggin' the fanny off 'er when this little sprog jumps on mi back and starts slappin' mi arse and shoutin', yippee! Faster, faster! Well, I'll tell you, mi dick went limp as a deflated balloon. It ruined what should 'ave been a night of passion.'

Jim stopped seeing the lady from the Crown when he contracted a dose of the clap, namely gonorrhoea, but with the number of assignations Jim had and given the promiscuity of the landlady it was anyone's guess who had given what to whom. There was no embarrassment to Jim, he had the skin of a pachyderm, and like the rest of us he carried on using the pub. The landlady left the pub not long after and a new manager moved in.

Whether she left of embarrassment or because of all the finger pointing and whispering, or not, is anyone's guess.

The Crown was a good pub which occasionally had live rock bands performing within its limited confines and it was here that I met Elaine, the girl I would later marry. We met about three weeks before I was sent to the BR road vehicle driving school and we married two years later and after 40 years we are still together.

Elaine and I used The Crown, sometimes, on a Saturday night and would go there as a foursome with Knocker and his girlfriend, Kathy. We still frequented the Crown after we were married.

CHAPTER 8
THE BIG 4

The first public railways were built as local rail links ran by small independent companies. In the early days little consideration was given to the potential for traffic, both passenger and goods. Most towns and villages had a rail connection and sometimes two or three. From the early 19th to the early 20th centuries most of these independent railway companies were either bought out or amalgamated until only a handful remained. These were known as the Big Four.

The Big Four were The Great Western Railway (GWR), The London and North Eastern Railway (L&NER), The London, Midland, Scottish Railway(LMS), and The Southern Railway (SR). Other lines operating as Joint Railways remained separate from the Big Four, these included The Midland and Great Northern Joint Railways and The Somerset and Dorset Joint Railways. The Big Four were Joint-stock, public companies.

During the Second World War the company's managements joined together, in effect forming a single railway company. After the war, for both practical and ideological reasons, the government decided to bring the rail service into the public sector.

THE GREAT WESTERN RAILWAY

Nicknamed 'God's Wonderful Railway' The Great Western (GWR) was created, via an act of Parliament, in 1835 to provide a double tracked line from Bristol to London. Work had begun in 1832 to research possible routes and stations and bridges etc. The engineer brought in to oversee construction was Isambard Kingdom Brunel. Construction started in 1836 at two locations, London to Reading and Bristol to Bath with each working towards the other. The terminal stations for this endeavour were London Paddington and Bristol Temple Meads.

Brunel decided that the tracks should be set at 7ft & 0¼ inch broad gauge rather than the 4ft 8½ inches standard gauge. His arguments for this were more comfort for passengers and faster running times.

The London - Bristol route was completed in 1841 and in 1843 the locomotive and carriage shed was opened at Swindon. Not long afterwards the loco works produced its first engine aptly named The Great Western. As the GWR spread its tendrils to cover all of the West Country parts of the broad gauge were replaced by standard gauge track.

Because the coal merchants and suppliers were dictating the price of coal and therefore the running costs, the company started its own mining operations in Blaenavon, Wales. This gave employment to 2500 miners and supplied the company with cheaper coal.

Construction of the Severn Tunnel started in 1873 and in 1892 the last of Brunel's broad gauge track was lifted and replaced.

THE LONDON & NORTH EASTERN RAILWAY

The L&NER was created in 1923 during the grouping of companies after The First World War due to shortage of finance brought about by the war. In Scotland it consisted of The North British Railway and The Great North of Scotland Railway. In

England it consisted of The North Eastern Railway, The Great Northern Railway, The Great Central Railway and The Great Eastern Railway. At one time it was nicknamed The 'Late and Never Early Railway.'

The L&NER produced several classes of locomotive, mainly to the designs of Nigel Gresley, including the 4468 Mallard, holder of the world's steam loco record. It also built the world famous 4472 Flying Scotsman.

THE LONDON, MIDLAND AND SCOTTISH RAILWAY

The London Midland and Scottish Railway (LMS) was formed in 1923 by the forced grouping of over 300 railway companies into just four after The First World War.

It was formed, mainly, from The Caledonian Railway, The Furness Railway, The Glasgow and South Western Railway. The Highland Railway, The London and North Western Railway including The Lancashire and Yorkshire Railway, The Midland Railway and The North Staffordshire Railway.

THE SOUTHERN RAILWAY

The Southern Railway is the smallest of The Big Four and is the only one confined solely to England and although it is the smallest its traffic is denser than any of the other rail companies. It too came into being with the forced grouping strategy.

The main framework of The Southern's system consists of four important railways, The London and South Western Railway, The London, Brighton and South Coast Railway, The South East and London Railway and The Chatham and Dover Railway plus other smaller lines. It is known as London's link to the South coast and controls the lion's share of cross Channel traffic. Unlike the other three companies, who derive a lot of their revenue from mineral, chemical and general goods traffic, the Southern generates ninety percent of its revenue from passenger traffic.

CHAPTER 9
A NEW DRIVER AT DEANSGATE

THE DRIVING SCHOOL

After about two months as a driver's mate on shift work, I was told that my application to go to Railway's Road Vehicle Driving School had been successful. I and two other lads from Deansgate were about to be trained as professional drivers. The two other lads were a half caste Afro/English guy called Stuart Onigbanjo and a chap named Johnny Olafson who was of Swedish descent. All three of us were to be trained in the Scammell Scarab, mechanical horse, urban articulated vehicle. At the same time three lads from Victoria were also going to be trained in the finer arts of driving, two of them in four wheel rigid vehicles and the third in a Scammell Scarab. Of the three guys from Victoria I only recall the name of one, he was the lad that was allocated the Scammell, and his name was Pete Oliver.

Pete Oliver was a Salford lad who rode a 650cc Motorcycle known as a Tribsa, which was a hybrid machine built from a pre unit Triumph Bonneville engine in a BSA Gold Star Frame. Although he was based at Victoria and I was based at Deansgate Pete became a good friend and knocked around with me and Knocker and our friends.

Peter was the drummer and lead singer in a group called The New Religion and he had played, with his group, in Germany at the same time as the Beatles. Upon returning to England he had got a job on the railway although he still played drums and sang with his group at weekends. During the 1970's the New Religion had a change of personnel and a change of name. Pete retained his position as the drummer and lead singer in the newly named Sweet Chariot. Sweet Chariot achieved some fame and made a few records and appeared numerous times on television. Peter eventually went solo but in the 1990's fate caught up with him and probably because of his heavy smoking habit; he was struck down with throat cancer. After going through all the medication and chemotherapy he was declared clear and he resumed his singing career.

Stuart Onigbanjo was a half caste African lad and a friend of mine and Knocker's and indeed we went out at weekends with our girlfriends together. Stuart's girlfriend was called Frances and with Elaine and me and Knocker and his girl Kathy we were quite inseparable and we all married our respective girlfriends within a couple of years of each other. Stuart left the railway within two years of passing his driving test, to take up employment with John Laing's Builders, where he prospered.

Johnny Olafson was a Collyhurst lad of Swedish descent who after passing his driving test stole regularly from his employers. He left the railway when his nefarious deeds were discovered. He was caught in the act and sentenced, with an accomplice, to a term in Wormwood Scrubs. His thieving activities had centred around the GUS return goods which he had sold on to a third party.

The first day at the driving school was an induction day was and once all the introductions had been carried out, we were assigned our training vehicles and began to familiarise ourselves with them. The second day was classroom based learning the theoretical side to driving. The third day was spent on the mechanical side including maintenance. The rest of the first week was spent in the yard practising gear changing, reversing and coupling and un-coupling trailers. The next three weeks were split so that two days were yard and classroom based and three days were out on the road. The last two weeks up until test day, on the Friday of the last week, were spent solely driving with just a break for dinner.

After the six weeks intensive tuition came the day of the test and on the day, out of the six Manchester lads, only one failed. The one failure was a Victoria employee who after three months applied again for the school. He was accepted and went through the same rigorous training for the second time, but this time with a different result, he passed.

Upon returning to Deansgate with our pass certificates we were congratulated on passing and asked for our provisional licenses and pass certificates. We handed them to the inspector to be sent to the licensing authority with the requisite fee, which the railways paid, and in return we each of us received a British Railway's Domestic Driver's License, which was immediately stamped SCARAB, SCAMMELL, 3 TON and signed and dated by the inspector. All we had to do now was to wait for our full licenses to be returned and even though we were allowed to drive on the domestic license, we didn't feel like professional drivers until we had the physical proof of the full license in our hands.

THE RAILWAY'S DOMESTIC LICENSE

Once we had our full licenses and over a period of time, we were required to take training on the different types of vehicle which we may have been required to drive. This meant going out for a day with a driver qualified in whichever vehicle the trainee was to be passed out on. Sometimes, the trainee was tested by a railway's driving instructor to assess his capability. Other times the trainee was sanctioned to drive whichever vehicle he had his day's training on by the Inspector.

The first of these vehicles to be stamped on my railway's domestic license, under the Scammell Scarab, was the petrol powered, six cylinder Bedford 'K' series which with the three ton Morris and the Karrier Bantam were the only vehicles, at the time, at Deansgate, to have synchromesh gearboxes. I passed out on the 4D Fordson Thames and the 3 ton Austin 'K' series within a couple of weeks of the Bedford.

The petrol powered Morris was the next vehicle to be stamped onto my domestic license and for this I was sent out with Gerry Mahoney, for a day. Gerry was the guy who had been forced into a retest because of his bad driving record. He told me to change down when there was no need and asked me why I had changed down to second to take certain corners. I actually drove to my own standards and not his, taking no notice of his instructions. Upon our return to the depot, Gerry had told Ernie Etchells that I was quite capable of driving the Morris. I was sanctioned to drive the Morris although I didn't, at that time, view a recommendation from Gerry as being anything to write home about.

The last vehicle I was tested on was the Dennis in which my training driver was Walter wall. The Dennis had a rear set gear lever mated to a constant mesh gear box. When changing up the box, especially in the Rolls Royce Diesel powered model, one had to de-clutch and knock the stick into neutral and wait for the revs to diminish so that the engine speed matched the road speed and then de-clutch again and slip it into the next higher gear. When changing down one had to rev, when in neutral, to match the road speed with the engine speed. This was the normal procedure in vehicles fitted with constant mesh gear boxes, but the revs dropped so slowly in this Dennis model that it was considered an unviable proposition to change up when climbing a hill, no matter how slight. The vehicle would have come to a stop before the next higher gear could be accommodated.

The Dennis F8 Pax, being an early 1950's vehicle had no electric signalling indicators and so one had to give hand signals. I was driving towards Mayfield Station, from Deansgate Depot, with Walter sat in the passenger seat giving me instruction. As we approached the first corner Walter said 'Right, let's change down, Clutch down! Into neutral! Clutch out! Rev! Signal! Clutch down! Third gear! Signal again!' And suddenly I found myself with my left hand on the gear lever and my right hand out of the window rotating in a signalling motion. Walt quickly grabbed the wheel and said, 'Fuckin' 'ell, who's driving this vehicle, you or me?'

Regaining the steering wheel from Walter I carried on towards Mayfield until Walt decided, in his wisdom, that he would tell me again, that it was time I changed up a gear, he said, 'Come on, Laurie, get it in top gear.'

I dipped the clutch, knocked the stick into neutral and waited for the revs to reach the right pitch. Unfortunately I got it wrong on this occasion and the stick was thrown back. Once again I dipped the clutch and pulled down on the rear set gear lever and attempted to slip it into top gear. The gear shaft pushed the gear cogs towards each other, but the spinning cogs were not aligned and amidst the crunching and grinding noises the gear stick was thrown back again. I'd lost it and in desperation I slammed it back down to find the gear. The stick once again met opposition and the cogs would not mesh and with a sharp crack, like the sound of Lash La Rue's bullwhip, the gear lever snapped off in my hand leaving the vehicle in neutral and me sat there with one hand on the steering wheel and an eighteen inch length of broken gear stick in my other hand. Walter sat in the passenger seat with his hands to his mouth, trying to stifle a laugh whilst I steered the disabled vehicle into the kerb. Luckily there was a public phone box quite near and I used it to summon the railways' breakdown vehicle to the rescue.

A pass on the Dennis was eventually achieved and thus, at the time, I had the full complement of vehicles on my domestic license.

DEMONSTRATING THE SCARAB TO THE YANKS

Not long after passing my driving test I was given a load to deliver to Exchange Station platform. The entrance to the section of platform I needed was mid way between Victoria Passenger station and Exchange Station. That platform was accessed by driving past the frontage of Victoria and turning left and driving along the roadway that ran parallel with the platform along this roadway were various bays that were sectioned off for parcels to different parts of the country. Some of these bays contained parcels for trains leaving Victoria and others held parcels for trains leaving Exchange.

I asked a porter where he wanted me to reverse my trailer. He pointed to the requisite bay and I started to reverse in. As I was reversing I heard a voice spoken in an American accent, 'Mah Gawd.' Said the male of the Yankee couple 'Would ya look at that?'

His female companion said, 'I've never seen anything like that back home.'

As I finished my manoeuvre the Americans came over to my cab and the male asked 'What d'ya call that there thing, man?'

I informed him about Mechanical Horses and in particular about the Scammell Scarab. He and his companion were intrigued by the British methods of local distribution and he ventured to speak once again, 'Ah'm a Long haul truck driver back home and believe me, we ain't never seen nuthin' like this. Mah wife and me, we're on vacation over here in Europe. Now, can I ask a favour of you?'

'Sure.' I replied 'Anything within reason.' It seemed that the Yanks considered us a part of Europe back in the sixties.

'Waal, ah'd be forever grateful to yuh if yuh could pull yer machine out, drive it around a little and reverse it back in that thur bay while mah lil ole wife here gets it on Super 8 film so's ah can show the boys back home.'

I did as requested and so I am set down for posterity on some American trucker's home movie. The Yanks were grateful and very happy, so happy in fact that the Yankee trucker delved in his pockets and produced a fiver and slipped it in my hand. They then swaggered off very pleased with themselves. I looked at the note in my hand in bewilderment. That fiver was half a week's basic pay to me back then.

IN HOT WATER

On one occasion, on a summer's day, I was allocated a rather dim van lad to work with, his name was Cuthbert Titterington, a slack jawed, chinless, half wit. He was neither the brightest star in the firmament or the sharpest knife in the drawer. He was a couple of cards short of a full deck to say the least. Not only was he slow of mind he was generally slow of action, until that day.........!

On that day we had loaded at Knightsbridge Cake with three tons of jam sponge cake, in a trailer which was being pulled by a Scammell Scarab, for tipping at Mayfield Station. On the return journey as we approached Mayfield I thought to myself 'It's getting a bit warm in this cab even for a hot summer's day.' It was then that I glanced at the temperature gauge and noticed that it was registering in the red zone. Glancing through my open window into my rear view mirror I noticed that there was steam issuing from the radiator cap, which was situated to the rear of the cab. I tentatively touched the radiator, which was situated inside the cab on the rear bulkhead and between the seats. It was blisteringly hot and I removed my hand immediately lest it should have been burned. I looked across the cab at Titterington; he was sat there mopping his brow which was sweating profusely and my thoughts continued, 'Poor silly bastard hasn't got the sense to open his window and let a breeze circulate within the cab. So I shouted to the imbecile, 'Hey, numb nuts! Open your bloody window!'

He started, awoken from his reverie by my shout, he looked at me and asked 'Why di'nt y'ask me earlier? I'm sweatin' like an idiot 'ere.'

'Quite right,' I thought, 'like a bloody idiot.' My next thought was that if I could get the vehicle up the station approach and onto the station proper, the vehicle would have time to cool down whilst it was unloaded. It would then be possible to attempt to find out what the problem was, replenish the radiator with coolant and if necessary drive the vehicle round to the workshops at North Western Street for inspection and repair.

The drive up the approach and onto the station was achieved without further problems, but upon parking the vehicle up on the platform, to start the unloading process, things started to go awry. Titterington had pulled his rubber work gloves on and as the vehicle had come to a halt the buffoon, unusually and with alacrity, jumped from the cab and made his way around to the offside of the vehicle where the radiator filler cap was located. His gloved hand reached for the filler cap and attempted, for reasons known only to himself, to remove it.

Upon realising what was about to occur, I exited the cab with all haste and attempted to grab hold of the simpleton and pull him away from the unit. As I reached for Titterington's arm I lost my footing and slipped and fell forward crashing into the van lad and spinning both of us around just as the filler cap came free. Boiling water gushed upwards and outwards and then cascaded downwards in a smaller imitation of the 'Old Faithful' geyser at Yellowstone National Park.

A few drops from the gusher splashed on both Titterington's and my hands and arms as we both fell backwards through the open doors of a half loaded railway carriage. We crashed into the pile of parcels and bounced back onto the platform landing in a heap on the floor. Luckily my unusually swift action and unplanned trip had saved the nincompoop from certain disfigurement and pain. If the boiling gusher of water had have spewed into his face and body he would have been terribly scalded and most certainly hospitalised.

After disentangling ourselves and resuming an upright position I gave the young idiot a ballocking for his foolhardy actions and he, with tears starting to well in his eyes, apologised for his actions, he said 'I'm sorry, I was on'y tryin' to help.' Good intentions without knowledge can lead to very serious consequences as Cuthbert Titterington almost found out. He would have really been in hot water.

The vehicle was then unloaded and I then set about finding out what the problem was. I got down on my hands and knees and attempted to look under the vehicle. I could not see much so I rolled onto my back and slithered under the vehicle. The problem soon came to light; it was a non existent fan belt, which had snapped and been lost.

The radiator was replenished with water and the vehicle was then slowly driven to the workshops where a repair was affected.

BOMBER

One of the trailer boys I worked with for a time was a lad named Brian (Bomber) Jackson. Bomber was seventeen years old at the time and he dressed in the popular rocker gear of the day. Most of the younger drivers and van lads had taken to wearing leather biker's jackets and denim jeans. A few of the younger lads sported Beatle hairstyles. These few modish youths cut their railway great coats up to jacket length and at this length they made very credible reefer jackets.

Bomber came from a railway family his elder brother Bob was an engine driver at Piccadilly Station and his father was an ex railwayman. Bomber's middle initial was R giving him the moniker BR Jackson.

Bomber was a very hirsute individual, he would come to work in the morning clean shaven and by the end of his shift he had the makings of a full beard. He would come to work the following day after having a shave but he would have left on what were then full grown sideburns.

He was forever pre-occupied with all things sexual. He bought all the soft porn magazines of the day such as Playboy, Men Only and Tit-Bits and read avidly the books of Frank Harris and The Marquis de Sade along with D.H. Lawrence's Lady Chatterley's Lover, John Cleland's Fanny Hill and the Indian love manual, The Kama Sutra and lesser pornographic novels like 'The Story of 'O' by Pauline Reage and the very sexually explicit Candy by Terry Southern, Mason Hoffenberg and Maxwell Kenton. He was also a fan of blue movies on Super 8 film and probably later on video cassettes or DVD.

For all his sexual predilections he was a good natured and humorous lad and he worked with me for a few months until he went to the driving school. On one occasion we were sent to pick up a load of parcels from Piccadilly. The parcels were stacked high on three or four of the pull along trucks which littered the platforms of all railway stations.

Once I had located the load and parked up Bomber climbed into the back of the trailer of the Scammell that we were using and I started throwing the parcels up to him to stack in the trailer. The second pull along had, sat on the top of the pile of parcels, a small box which I struggled to reach. I finally got a grip of the box and without looking I tossed it into the back of the trailer. It tumbled over and over as it flew through the air. Butterfingers Bomber failed to catch the box and it fell, upside down, to the floor of the trailer with a loud avian screeching issuing from it.

It was at this point that we realised that the box contained a racing pigeon that had been inadvertently left on the pull along truck. Bomber picked up the box and looked at me with a wide grin on his face, and said. 'That's the first bird I've ever seen that could fly without using its wings. It needs to brush up on its landing technique though.'

I sent Bomber, with the homing bird, to the livestock office to book the pigeon in and leave it with the livestock personnel. Luckily it seemed none the worse for its unexpected, assisted flight.

If I had time, and one usually had on the railways, during the day I would call round to my girl friend's house in Crown Street, Salford, around about dinner time. Bomber would accompany me. One particular day we arrived as she was stood outside. Her mother had gone out shopping and Elaine, home from work for her dinner, had forgotten her key.

An open, upstairs window was spotted by Bomber and he suggested that I drive the van onto the pavement close to the wall of the property and that he would climb onto the roof of the van, climb through the bedroom window and come downstairs and open the front door. Foolishly we agreed that this was the way forward and so I positioned the vehicle as Bomber suggested and he climbed onto the roof. As he attempted to climb through the bedroom window one of his flailing feet, encased in a size nine, steel toe capped boot came into contact with the large pane of glass which was the main window. A crack appeared and with its various tributaries, quickly travelled along the glass pane from bottom to top.

Struggling, as he was, to get his none too slim bulk through the opening light, he became stuck fast. There was just his arse and his legs on the outside the rest of his body was dangling on the inside and he was searching frantically with his hands for some kind of purchase to pull himself through.

By this time passers by and some neighbours had gathered around. People were pointing while others offered suggestions and others just laughed at Bomber's predicament. It was then that I decided to give Bomber a helping hand. I climbed onto the roof of the vehicle, took one of Bomber's feet in each hand and started to wiggle him from side to side whilst pushing forwards. All of a sudden his feet were snatched from my hands as my attempts to extricate him came to fruition. His rump had slid through the gap and then his not inconsiderable weight had taken over. His upper body being in a position lower than the rest of him, gravity did its job and Bomber fell through the open light and onto a bedside table with a resounding crash, scattering ornaments, toiletries, scent bottles and the table itself in all directions. He ended up on the bed then rolled off pulling the eiderdown on top of himself. I shouted 'Bomber! Are you all right?'

'I fuckin' will be when I get out of this bleedin' eiderdown.' Came the reply.

With utmost haste I climbed down to ground level but when I got there Bomber, light on his feet considering his lack of athletic qualities and his weight, had already dashed downstairs and opened the front door. He said, 'Come on, let's bugger off before her mum comes home or we're for it.'

'Right oh' I replied. 'Let's go!' I said ta-ra to Elaine who assured me she'd sort everything out and that she would phone me when it was safe for me to show my face again. I got into the van started it up and returned to Deansgate Depot, where Bomber immediately found an audience for his latest escapade.

By the weekend Elaine had phoned me and told me that she had explained things to her mother and that everything was OK. Even so, I thought it wise not to visit her house for a few days. By the following week and having built up the courage, like St George, I decided to face the dragon and along, to offer moral support, came Bomber.

Parking the railway's, 'K' series, petrol powered, six cylinder Bedford outside the terraced house on Crown Street, Bomber and I got out to face the music. I knocked, rather tentatively upon the door and waited until the door opened and I was confronted by the future Mother in Law. 'Hello boys.' She said, smiling disarmingly 'Won't you come in?'

We entered and sat down, me by Elaine and Bomber in a chair facing the television. The feared matriarch went into the kitchen to brew a pot of tea. She returned a few minutes later with a tray containing four mugs of tea and a plate of biscuits which she placed on the parlour table. She then sat down between Elaine and me. 'Right.' She said 'What, exactly, occurred on your last visit? My daughter here said that she managed to crack the upstairs window while cleaning up and that she fell onto the table, breaking it. Although I was a little doubtful that a seven stone girl could cause that much damage, I believed her. That was until I saw the big oily boot mark on the eiderdown. Then I met one of my neighbours who told me a completely different story, backed up, of course, by various other neighbours who witnessed your shenanigans.'

My apology came hesitantly. 'I-I-I don't know what to say. We were only trying to help, I'm terribly sorry. It won't happen again.' I said. But then I noticed she was smiling.

'That was worth it,' she said 'just to see you trying to wheedle your way out of it and God, the look on your face just then.'

Elaine's mother was a divorcee whose husband had had an affair and left his wife and 3 children to set up home with his floozy. The single mum was now courting a Dutch seaman, a bit of a handyman about the house, who, while docked at Salford, had called around and re- glazed the window and repaired any damage done. I'd gotten away with it.

Our tea and biscuits finished we bade the mother and daughter good bye and went out to the wagon. Clambering into the vehicle I noticed that the key was no longer in the ignition where I had foolishly left it. That's when I heard a tap on the driver's door. I opened the door to be confronted by one of Elaine's neighbours. A man of about forty years of age was stood before me waving the ignition key in my face. 'Looking for this, are you?' He asked. 'Well, I am just about Bloody well fed up of you and your bloody truck parked here every other bloody day, so if you want to drive away now, you'll have to phone your bloody depot for a spare bloody key and explain to them what your doing parked up where you shouldn't be and when you should be bloody working.'

'Come on, mate, don't mess about. Give us the key.'

'No bloody way' he said. 'Phone your bloody depot.'

The ensuing argument brought Elaine and her mother out to see what was going on. They pleaded with the neighbour to return the key, but got the same *'bloody'* response that I had received.

As this argument was progressing Elaine's uncle, her mother's brother John, came around the corner. Big John as he was known was in his mid thirties a bit younger than the guy that had my key, but there any similarity ended. John was well over 6 feet tall and well built. He lived like a Romany gypsy in a twenty five feet caravan with etched windows and chromium trimmings. He was what is known as a hard case and it wasn't long before John had gotten a grip on the man with the key. He grabbed his arm with one hand and his throat with the other, pinned him against the wall and said; 'Now, you wouldn't like to see these young men get into any trouble because of your actions, would you? And I don't really want to do you any harm, do I? So let us come to some amicable arrangement, shall we? Return the key and nothing gets broken!'

Within seconds I had my key back. I thanked Big John, said good bye to Elaine and her mother and drove away. No more problems were experienced with the key stealing neighbour whenever I parked in Crown Street after that day. Mind, I did, after that incident, and on other occasions, remove the key and lock the cab doors. No point in tempting providence, was there?

After a while Bomber went to the railway's driving school and passed his test. He like a few other drivers stuck it out on the railway until he had gotten his all group's license when, at the age of twenty one he left the railway and went into general haulage. He ended up returning into the fold of the railway's associated companies when he started work for Freightliner in the 1990's.

FREE CIGS FOR ALL

I had the pleasure to work with many and various van lads and trailer boys after Bomber, including some rogues from Salford, one or two of who later became drivers. These Salfordians, all from the Ordsall area, always had plenty of cash on them, considering the low wages that they were paid. It turned out that these youths had found a unique method of emptying outdoor cigarette vending machines that proliferated outside retail premises in the 60's. At the time most cigarettes cost less than a half crown for a pack of ten or if they were slightly more expensive a vending pack of nine was installed in the machine.

The method employed to pilfer from those automatic vendors was to tape a length of cotton to a half crown piece (12 ½ new pence) and deposit it into the machine. When the coin had dropped onto the trip mechanism within the machine it was pulled back ever so slightly and taped into place. This left the trip mechanism activated and allowed each column of ciggies to be emptied in turn. With each pack of cigs that was liberated came the change, down a separate tube. When all the cigarettes and change had been extracted, the tape was removed from the thread which was holding the coin; the coin then fell into the machine to be rejected because the machine was empty, thus allowing the same coin to be used over and over.

The knowledge of this malpractice within the younger element of the railway staff at Deansgate led to a spate of thefts all over Manchester resulting in the law enforcement body publishing a piece in the local newspapers to the effect that 'Thieves have found an ingenious method of emptying cigarette machines in the Manchester area and the police are, at present, at a loss to what this method is.'

The liberation of cigarettes and change continued until the price of a pack of ten rose above 2s/6d (12 ½ new pence) and the half crown coin could not be used. Nobody, that I knew of, was apprehended whilst perpetrating this crime and the police never, as far as I was aware, discovered the method used.

Another incident concerning the cigarette machines happened one Friday night when a Deansgate driver and his van lad, who shall remain nameless, came out of the Crown public house, at approximately 2000hrs to do their last trip of their late shift from Victoria.

Just a hundred yards or so from the crown was a row of shops on Victoria Street. One of these shops was a lock up, newsagents which was, at that time of the evening, closed and bereft of staff. Positioned outside was a cigarette machine containing half a dozen columns of different brands of cigarettes. An opportunity, was spotted by the driver and his nipper, to make some money quickly, by relieving the machine of all its goods and cash.

The vehicle was parked up outside the shop and when the coast was clear they alighted and approached the machine. In his hand the driver held, with the requisite length of cotton taped to it, a Half Crown piece which he deposited in the payment slot. The coin was pulled back the tiny amount needed and taped into place. The first drawer was pulled open and the cigarettes removed but as the driver slammed the drawer shut the Sellotape holding the cotton came unstuck and the coin fell into the machine, bringing to an end their hopes of an easy killing.

In exasperation the youth drew back his leg which terminated in a foot enclosed in a steel, toe-capped, work boot. He kicked out in fury at the legs that supported the machine and shook it violently. The machine, under the force of the kick and the shaking, moved backwards a few inches and one of the retaining bars holding it in place fell away. The lad then pushed the other side of the machine and the other retaining bar fell away leaving the machine free standing.

Driver and van lad looked at each other and started to laugh and an immediate tacit agreement as to what was to be done next was reached. The tailboard of the vehicle was dropped and the whole machine, which with its legs was close to six feet high, was manhandled into the back of the vehicle and the vehicle was then driven to Deansgate Depot.

Once in the depot the truck was driven to an out of the way spot at the top of the yard. The two thieves then threw the machine out of the back of the van and on to the cobbles where, upon landing, the glass at the front of the machine smashed and then aided by a couple of loose cobblestones and plenty of enthusiasm the machine was viciously attacked. Within fifteen minutes all the cigarettes and cash had been extracted.

The empty, wrecked machine, which was by then much lighter, was thrown back onto the vehicle which was driven to Castlefield Wharf where it was thrown, quickly into the Bridgewater Canal. At first, perhaps because of the air within it, the otherwise empty machine refused to sink. The two buffoons that were responsible for the perpetration of this crime started to throw objects at the machine in an attempt to expedite its demise.

They were still throwing stones at the slowly sinking machine when sirens were heard and the headlights of a blue and white, police panda car came into view. The two nefarious plonkers ran to their vehicle and jumped in. The police car, a Ford Anglia, pulled up in front of their vehicle and two Bobbies got out and made their way to the driver's side of the railway vehicle. The policeman who seemed to be in charge addressed the occupants, 'How long have you been here, boys?'

' A couple of minutes. We've just pulled up for a brew.' The driver replied holding up his Thermos flask.

'You haven't seen anything suspicious, have you?'

'No, nothing. Why? What's up?'

'Well, we've had a report of someone throwing a large object into the canal.' The officer replied.

'Well no ones been here since we pulled up, but there again, the wharf's a big place.' The driver replied.

'O.K. lads we'll have a look round. Enjoy your brew, good night now.'

'Good night officers.' Said the driver as both he and his lad took deep breaths of relief before heading back to Victoria for their last load.

Funnily, other than what became a good story within the confines of Deansgate Depot, nothing more was heard of the liberated and then drowned cigarette machine.

THE BOYS FROM SALFORD

The lads that started at Deansgate that came from Salford were a motley crew. Three of them started about a year before the ciggy gang. John Quill was a year younger than me and he stayed with the railways and went to the driving school where he passed on a Scammell Scarab. Upon reaching twenty one years of age and obtaining his all groups license he left to go into general haulage.

I met up with John a few years later when he got a job at Freightliner, Trafford Park and again when we both worked for Brain Haulage.

On the same day as John Quill started another lad from the Ordsall area also started. His name was Tommy Cunliffe and a week later a lad called Harold Donaldson started. Harold was eighteen years of age when he started and he came to work on a 650cc pre unit Triumph Bonneville. His parents owned a hardware shop in Salford and Harold had aspirations to do the same. He left the railway after about eighteen months and with his parents help opened a shop outside the Manchester area. These three youths were sent by the Salford Youth Employment Office to fill the vacancies which none of them really wanted.

Those that started a year later all came from the Ordsall area of Salford and had all attended Ordsall Secondary Modern School. One of them George Jones had left on the same day as the others but was a year older because he had stayed on to gain a number of GCE's. One of the GCE's he had gained was in art and when he felt the urge would draw caricatures of various railway staff.

George stayed with the railway and obtained his driving license in a Scammell. He was quite a good friend and after I got married he would often call round to our marital home with his girl friend. He left the railway to take up employment with a crane hire company in a managerial position. Not long after that I lost touch with George.

Eddie English was a strange name for a lad who seemed to have so little command of the language Eddie became Big Roger's nipper for a time and I believe it may have been he that was responsible for the escaped porker mentioned earlier. It was while he was with Roger that he skipped a day's work. The following day I was chatting to Eddie and I asked 'How come you weren't in work yesterday?'

'Well,' he replied 'mi mam wasn't well an' I 'ad to go t't Doctor's sugary for 'er transcription for some depositories.'

'What?' I asked, looking somewhat puzzled, 'What's up with her?'

'She's got dese adenoids, dem's piles yuh know an' she's got tuh shove dese depositories up 'er plectrum, dat's 'er bum yuh know, but dat's better dan las' year when she t'ought she was 'avin' an 'eart attack an' it turned out she on'y had a cute vagina. She's always ill, she's a bloody kleptomaniac.

Eddie used these inappropriate words and malapropisms all the time, whether by accident or design no one could tell.

Eddie was joker by nature and one time he and Roger had pulled up on Canal Street for their dinner. Eddie got out of the vehicle and sat on the canal wall to eat his sandwiches. Suddenly he jumped up and shouted 'Help! Roger! Mi mate's fell in the canal!'

Laurie Driver

Roger, dozing in the driver's seat, was taken completely unawares; he jumped from the vehicle and ran round to Eddie who was still shouting 'Mi mate! Mi mate!'

Rog grabbed hold of Eddie and said 'What're you on about, your mate's not here.'

'No, not mi mate like mi best pal.' Eddie said very calmly, 'Mi mate off mi butty, yer know mi mate, like mi roast beef.' He then started laughing and said, 'I had yer goin' there, didn't I, big feller.'

Lastly, there was Charlie Axon, a bit of a hard case whose dad was a docker. Charlie would fight anyone at the drop of a hat. I remember one occasion when I, Knocker, Charlie and George Jones, who on this occasion was my van lad, as Charlie was Knocker's, went, at dinner time, to the Haymarket pub for a pie and a pint. We were almost finished when Charlie, wiping his mouth with the back of his hand, rose from his seat and walked around the table to where George was sat. George, last to finish, had at the time, half a meat and potato pie, liberally laced with tomato ketchup, raised to his mouth, about to take a bite. With no warning and for no apparent reason Charlie drew back his arm, bunched his fist and WALLOP! He thumped George in the side of the head. The pie was wiped across George's face before it flew from his hand, describing an arc through the air prior to hitting the wall and sliding down to the dado rail and tumbling to the floor, leaving a greasy, red and brown gravy stain in its wake. George tumbled sideways, his face bespattered by the remnants of the pie and its tomato sauce dressing, landing in a heap beside the table. I leapt to my feet as did Knocker; just as Charlie drew back is foot, as if about to take a penalty, with George's head. Knocker went to help George, who was a bit dazed, not to say puzzled and I grabbed Charlie by the shoulders and spun him around and pushed him into the seating. I shouted 'Fuckin' 'ell Chas! What yer doing?'

130

'I've always wanted to batter that clever bastard.' He replied.

'Well this isn't the time or the place.'

At that moment, Dougie, the landlord came into the room to find out what all the commotion was about. I tried to explain as best I could, what had transpired between those erstwhile school friends. I had persuaded them to shake hands and asked Charlie to apologise for his stupid act of violence which he did quite graciously considering what he obviously thought of George. Dougie gave us all a lecture and banned both the van lads from the pub. Luckily George sustained only a bruise from that encounter and he and Charlie kept their distance after that.

Charlie left the railway after a few months because his dad had gotten him a job on the docks, although this wasn't destined to be a long career either as the docks started down staffing in the run up to eventual closure.

AN INDUSTRIAL ACCIDENT

It was during my first year as a driver and I was covering Jake's round while he was on annual leave. The delivery rounds were now worked by a driver without a trailer boy or van lad because the majority of the delivery drivers, in their wisdom, had accepted a slightly higher pay rise than the norm to work on their own. That rise, was in fact a bribe, a form of inveiglement, a cost cutting exercise that the greedier drivers accepted and those, like Jake, who were a little more forward looking voted against, but as is human nature, greed defeated common sense. The van lads/trailer boys were sold down the river, by the drivers, for a small raise which would soon be eroded away much like the conductors on the buses would later be thrown out of work for the same reasons when their drivers thought they were capable of routinely doing the conductor's job whilst driving a bus.

I was on a 6-2 shift for the first week that Jake was off and I was told to come in for my rostered shift and complete a run from Mayfield to Victoria and back to Deansgate using Jake's vehicle and then load up for the delivery round. My van lad would be found other work or continue the rest of his shift with another driver.

Once I had loaded up for the delivery round I went to Oldham Road Goods Depot Canteen for breakfast. There I met other drivers and porters. We conversed and ate a hearty, subsidised breakfast. By this time it was about 0930hrs and so I started my deliveries of which I only had a few.

One of my deliveries was to an old mill on Marlborough Street, which then housed a number of clothing firms. The Marlborough Street Mill was just off Hulme Street one block back from and running parallel with Oxford Street.

What happened in the next few minutes I put into the 50-50-99 category. That is to say that if there is a fifty-fifty chance that you will get something right then there is a ninety nine per cent probability that it will go wrong. And it did.

Driving into the yard I spun the little Scammell artic around and reversed down the cobbled yard to the designated unloading area. After parking the vehicle I alighted and went to the rear of the trailer where I dropped the tail board and threw up the roller shutter. I then climbed into the trailer and picked up the large but light parcels that I had to deliver. The parcels that I carried contained the latest fashions in lady's clothing and were piled higher than my eyes. It seems, in hindsight, a fair probability that I misjudged the distance to the end of the trailer and I walked off the edge into thin air. Now, never having sprouted wings or learned the art of levitation, I fell to the floor rather suddenly, landing in an untidy heap and badly twisting my left ankle between two cobblestones. As I fell the parcels were strewn, in a random pattern, around me.

At first, those people that were present in the yard seemed to find a great deal of mirth in my show of aerial acrobatics and, no doubt, my stupidity. Their reaction changed to one of concern when they realised that the figure writhing around on the floor, in agony before, them wasn't quite the humorous spectacle that it at first appeared and within seconds people were milling around me, enquiring as to my condition and trying to administer to me in whichever way they thought best. Some kind individual brought out a wooden chair for me to sit on as the cobbles were somewhat hard, uncomfortable and unforgiving.

I was helped up and assisted, hopping on my good leg, to the chair. As I sat on the seat, still in severe pain, I was aware of someone removing my boot. As the boot came free from my swollen foot I let out something between a scream and a whimper. The circumference of my ankle, by then, was akin to the distance around a large cantaloupe melon and was throbbing incessantly.

Mary, the forelady in charge of the company I was delivering to, made a phone call to Deansgate Depot and also dialled for an ambulance. While I waited for the ambulance to arrive I filled in the companies Accident Report Book. As I finished the report Inspector Etchells drove into the yard, with him was Knocker who had come to take over the deliveries and collections that I could no longer do.

The ambulance arrived and I was taken to Manchester Royal Infirmary where, believing I had only badly sprained my ankle, I would have it strapped up, be plied with analgesics and sent home to rest with my ankle in an elevated position. But no, I was put into a wheelchair and pushed into a cubicle where an angel in blue cut off my sock, revealing the swollen joint in all its discoloured and tumescent glory. The skin seemed to be stretched so tightly over my ankle that it appeared translucent like a water filled balloon that was about to burst. The ankle bone on either side of the foot seemed to have been swallowed up by creeping corpulence. There were a few ooh's and aah's from the nurse and a porter before I was wheeled down to the X-ray department where the Cathode rays discovered by Mr. Wilhelm Konrad Roentgen, (1845–1923) were used to detect and diagnose a fracture and torn ligaments and tendons within my ankle.

These X-ray snapshots were held up to a light box and the specialist viewing them, after a sharp intake of breath, related to me that an operation was needed to repair the ligaments and tendons and to reset the ankle bones and that I would spend the next week on a surgical ward.

I was then ferried down to the operating theatre where a pre-med was administered. After the pre-med had taken effect and I was feeling pleasantly drunk, light headed and giggling to myself, the full anaesthetic was given and I floated off into the realm of dreamland.

Consciousness returned to me a few hours later on a surgical ward where I was in terrible pain, dry mouthed and feeling nauseous. Sensibility came and went periodically and in one of my lucid moments a nurse gave me a lemon flavoured mouth swab. This made me feel a little better, but I could not face anything to eat until the next day when I awoke with a hunger so fierce I would have eaten a scabby horse, but far worse than that, there was only hospital food available. I spent a week in hospital and over four months off work, but before I was discharged. Training was given on how to perambulate with the aid of crutches

Instruction was given on the correct way to proceed up and down stairways, using those awkward walking aids. (I came close to breaking numerous other bones during this process). The plaster cast was changed a few times during the following weeks to necessitate the removal of stitches and the cleaning up of the post operative site and I had to attend the physiotherapy clinic once a week for six weeks after the cast was removed for good.

After I had been released from the hospital and sent home to recuperate I was visited by Joe O' Heeney, Knocker and Mitch and one or two others who took the time to come and see how I was faring. Inspector Etchell's also visited and he brought along with him the Deansgate Parcels Depot Accident Report Book which had to be filled in to conform to the health and safety rules of the day. I duly filled in the accident book and also registered my accident with the Social Services. There was no sick pay payable to me from the company and so I had to register it with the Social Services to enable me to get the higher rate of pay from them for accidents which occur within the workplace.

Before the aforementioned accident occurred my girlfriend and I had decided to get engaged, so when I returned to work, I started to put out feelers about jobs in general haulage for the time when I reached twenty one years of age, in order to seek better paid employment to enable us to save for our impending wedding.

THE BULLION RUN

There was one job that I did as both a van lad and as a driver, that job was known as the bullion run and was a task highly valued by both drivers and mates. The job entailed driving to Piccadilly Station, in a convoy of two or three railway vehicles, where a police escort would be awaiting us. Among the number of policemen in attendance were a number of armed officers.

Once at Piccadilly the lead vehicle would reverse onto the railway carriage and the driver, van lad and station porters would start to transfer a number of large chests which were full of bank notes or coinage that had been taken out of circulation and were bound for destruction. Each vehicle would be loaded in turn and before each was sealed up an armed officer would take up his position in the rear of the vehicle.

When all the vehicles were loaded and sealed they would then be driven to The Bank of England in Tib Lane near Albert Square.

On route a police motorcyclist outrider would lead the convoy. His job was to ensure that the convoy would not be stopped by anything as trivial as traffic lights on red. Obviously we could not afford to stop considering the cargo we carried. This was the same type of cargo that the great train robbers made history in stealing.

Behind the outrider followed a high powered police saloon car then the Railway vehicles. Behind the Railway convoy was another high powered saloon followed by another Motorcyclist. We drove non stop to the Bank of England where the vehicles were driven into the bank's yard and backed onto the loading bay to be unloaded.

When the unloading had taken place each of the drivers and mates were given a five shillings (twenty five new pence) gratuity for a job well done. Whether the police personnel and the railway porters were tipped I don't know.

When I did the bullion run as a driver's mate the bank was situated, as stated, on Tib Lane, but when I did the job as a driver the bank had moved to a new address between Portland Street and Moseley Street off York Street.

There was a tale going around at the time, although I did not witness the occurrence or swear to its validity, of an armed officer discharging his weapon accidentally on Piccadilly Station. I believe this happened when a driver, who had an interest in weaponry, asked the officer to show him his firearm. Although the officer should not have withdrawn the pistol he did so and it went off. It apparently discharged downwards into the ground and ricocheted down the empty platform and probably down the exit line. Due to the platform being used solely for the loading of the bullion no one was injured. I have no idea what would have happened to the policeman due to these circumstances, but I suppose he would have been grounded whilst an internal investigation was carried out and he was probably removed from firearms duty for good or, at least, the foreseeable future from that time.

THE ALL GROUPS LICENSE

A decision to carry on working for the railway until I attained the age of 21 seemed a good idea at the time. I would then get my all groups license which would allow me to drive all classes of vehicle.

The all groups license was the forerunner of the HGV license or LGV license. The difference being that no real test was needed to drive larger, heavier vehicles. Once the age of twenty one was reached, the all groups license was issued and if one applied for a job driving the heavier, larger vehicles, the company, to whom the application had been made, would send the applicant out with another company driver or manager to assess his or her capabilities. It was not until the 4th of August 1969 that the HGV test was adopted. The case to qualify for the new HGV license by Grandfather Rights was that a driver had to be driving the class of vehicle for which the license was required for at least six months between the months of August 1969 and July 1970. This requirement being satisfied, the license was granted.

Three weeks prior to my twenty first birthday Elaine and I married. Four weeks later, upon being the recipient of the All Groups License, I left Deansgate Depot and the Railways to seek my fortune in the world of General Haulage. I was about to become an itinerant. Although it would not be long before I returned to the fold and the security of the railways.

CHAPTER 10
JOB AFTER JOB

After leaving the railways I tried my hand at tipper driving for the O'Sullivan Bros of Store Street beneath Piccadilly Station. I didn't reign long because, due to my lack of experience on tippers, I was snapping half shafts like pencils. My next foray into general haulage was with Bridgewater Transport which was on Jake Barlow's delivery round. Bridgewater had a depot by the side of the Bridgewater Canal where it connects with the Irwell navigation via Pomona Dock and the Rochdale Canal at Castlefield, accessed via a yard off Egerton Street in Hulme. Their fleet consisted mainly of Atkinson Borderers powered by the Gardner 180 diesel. I handed my notice in after a couple of weeks when my brother in law phoned me to tell me of a vacancy at Barratt's meat haulage.

I took the job working for Barratt's who also had contracts with SPD grocery suppliers and also worked on the Harris Contract delivering all Mars products. I Left Barratt's after a few months because I had heard that there were massive wages to be earned as a private hire driver. I did a number of months as a taxi driver for Badger's cabs, working up to eighteen hours a day. The earnings were high but there was no time to spend them; it was all work and sleep. Taxi's, in my mind, should be fitted with tachographs and drivers of those vehicles should be regulated and monitored as stringently as LGV drivers to ensure some kind of restriction over the excessive hours worked by cabbies.

I returned to haulage with MAT Transport based in the Manchester International Freight Terminal (MIFT), pulling containers. I was sacked after two days for ripping most of the front off an Atki Borderer. I then heard that good money could be earned working for W. E. Hall's, also known as J.B. Carriers of Salford, working off Salford Docks, delivering newsprint to the Daily Express. The vehicles used were KM Bedford's fitted with the Detroit Diesel with thirty three feet, flat bed semi trailers. The promise of good money never materialised.

Kendal Milne's was the next company I sold my expertise to, delivering furniture all over the North West, from there I moved to Holt's brewery as a driver Drayman. I left before I became a dedicated sot. My next job was with a company called Storey Bros carrying railway axles, wheels and bogies and where each driver was issued with two log books, one legal and one actual. Oswald Ingham was my next employer Oswald was an independent haulier based in Newton Heath who ran a mixed fleet on container haulage. The company no longer exists.

Another job I took was with the Co-op on Briscoe Lane, Newton Heath delivering to Co-op depots from Carlisle to Hackney Wick. From there I went to a company called Paul Backhouse delivering motor factors. Three months of the same trip, same depots, same routes, same terminal boredom day after day.

CHAPTER 11
BACK TO THE RAILWAY

By that time it was 1970 and I realised that there was no future in chasing the big money and working for a couple of months here and a couple of months there for numerous companies. What I needed was some stability and permanence in my life and so I applied for a job with the railway once again. The vacancy that was on offer at the time was a class one driving position at Liverpool Road Goods Depot with what was now, since 1969, called NCL a subsidiary of Railfreight. All the vehicles were now painted in the new National Carriers and Railfreight livery of yellow. I took the job on offer.

The job was delivering bulk loads locally. All the loads were on flat bed trailers so each load had to be roped and sheeted and one would do between two and four loads a day depending upon where one was delivering. There was a bottom yard situated beneath the upper Liverpool road depot. The entrance to this lower yard was off Water Street and was used for storing loaded trailers. Liverpool Road Depot also had its own bonded warehouse for imports and exports of tobacco and alcoholic spirits. The Bond was manned by Custom's and Excise staff with help from the Liverpool Road porters.

It was nice to be back in the fold and to enjoy the camaraderie that seemed to permeate throughout the railways. The prime mover vehicles at Liverpool Road station were TK Bedford's fitted with the Scammell automatic coupling. They grossed out at twenty tons, giving a twelve tons pay load. The trailers were loaded either straight from the trains or from transit sheds. When the drivers started in the mornings their trailers would be loaded by the night staff and when a driver returned for a second load he would drop the trailer and pick up another ready loaded trailer which had been loaded by the porters or loading gangs. Only on rare occasions would a driver have to load his own trailer.

Albert Robinson, a driver at Liverpool Road Depot, when in a rush to get his second load jumped onto the flat bed of his trailer and acted as the receiver for the crane driver. As the crane driver lowered whatever the load consisted of, the receiver swung the crane's chains and what they were holding into position, onto the trailer and released the grabs or hooks and signalled the crane driver to raise the grabs away from the trailer.

On the day in question Albert was loading a cargo of bales which were lowered using grabs which had, as part of their structure, pointed protrusions to grip the bales. He was doing all right and almost had the trailer loaded, at three high and a binder, when, as he released the grabs and held them steady to stop them swinging around and after signalling the crane driver to take the grabs away he suddenly let out a high pitched yell. One of the steel protrusions on the grabs had caught beneath his wedding ring. By the time the crane driver realised what had occurred and before he could stop the crane Albert's body had took the full weight and he was hoisted aloft by his ring finger. Something had to give and unfortunately it was flesh and bone that was weakest at this point and Albert's finger was ripped bloodily and painfully from his hand at the knuckle.

Albert, a Salford man, was taken to hospital but the knuckle was too badly damaged and the finger could not be re-attached. He was off work for a couple of months and returned to work, minus his ring finger, and was put on light duties for a while. Whether he received anything in the way of compensation, I don't know. He was still working at Liverpool road when I left, but the depot closed not long after.

Most of the other drivers at Liverpool Road were getting close to pensionable age. There was Solly Andrews who was over sixty when I started and Tommy burns who was in his mid fifties and Jimmy Prendergast who was also close to retirement age. One of the drivers closer to my age was called Ken and a few years, after the closure of Liverpool Road, I saw him driving a four wheeler for a timber delivery firm and there was another guy called Tommy who I later saw, around about the same time, working in Trafford Park for a vehicle hire company. Another driver that worked at Liverpool road, while I was there was an Irish guy called Billy Brougham who lived in the Collyhurst area of Manchester. There were one or two more but, after the passage of a number of years, their names elude me.

A YACHTS MAST

One summer's day, when work was a little slack, I was given the job of delivering a thirty five feet long, yachts mast to Hollingworth Lake near Rochdale. I was not aware that there were yachts big enough to carry a thirty five feet mast at the Hollingworth Lake Marina, but that was what I had to load and deliver. I loaded the long, slim article of freight on to a short trailer and secured it with rope, using a variation of the barrel hitch. The mast overhung the rear of my trailer by about six feet and so I tied a bit of red rag to the end of it as a warning to following vehicles.

The depot actually had, in its possession, long load markers which were of a triangular shape with red edgings and a red stripe through the triangle diagonally. These were to be fitted on the end of any load that projected from the rear of the trailer, more than four feet. However these had been put in a place of safety by the driver foreman, Solly Andrews. So safe was this place that Solly had forgotten where it was and look high and low as we did we could not find the marker boards. Hence the red rag which had a dual purpose:

1: To serve as a warning to following vehicles so as to avoid a rear end collision.

2: To distract any enraged bulls that might be attacking pedestrians.

Once the red rag was attached I made my way to Hollingworth Lake. Upon reaching the vicinity of the lake I asked a local the whereabouts of the Marina Club House. I was told that it was on the opposite side of the lake a quarter of a mile down a single lane track which ran through a wooded area. The guy giving me directions assured me that the access was good and that there was plenty of room to turn my vehicle around. He used the words that we drivers are used to hearing and which puts us in a doubting frame of mind. These words being, 'They've had much bigger vehicles than yours down there.'

The access road was of the type driver's dread. It seemed to get narrower and narrower the further one drove down it. The club house came into view as branches, twigs and vines were trying to invade my cab like John Wyndham's Triffids' bent on destruction. The car park was full and there was only room for cars to turn around by way of executing a three point turn. If the car park had been empty there would still not have been enough room to swing my unit and trailer around. I would only have been able to get out of the car park by doing a couple of shunts.

After much searching, I finally found someone willing to accept responsibility for the delivery and who would commit his signature to paper. Once this was done and the mast was off loaded I asked if there was an alternative exit road other than the one I had entered by. There was none. It was impossible to turn around and so I had to reverse out along the quarter of a mile of woodland track that I had driven in on. The track had numerous blind bends and I knew that I would experience a little difficulty performing this task. Still, there was no other way I was going to get out of there, so I got into my cab, fired her up, selected reverse gear and started the process of egress from the predicament that I was in.

As I reversed around the first blind bend, the branches and twigs, once again, banged against the windshield and side windows. Tendrils of vine like plants seemed as if they were trying to tear the rear view mirrors off the vehicle. After much struggling I came to a small clearing where the undergrowth was low and there was a gap in the trees that was just wide enough to admit my trailer, if I reversed in using the utmost care.

My considered opinion was that the flattening of a few nettles, saplings and various other specimens of flora to enable me to turn around and drive out was well worth the effort, That decided I endeavoured to reverse into the space that I had selected and I had gone about twenty feet backwards when the back axle of my trailer dropped into a steep declivity and disappeared up to the hubs in mud.

Curses and oaths issued from my mouth before I calmed down and gathered my faculties. Realising what needed to be done I then engaged the differential lock, engaged a low gear and attempted to drive forward. This tactic was the only ploy open to me, other than having to resort to employing somebody to pull me out using a four wheel drive vehicle or a tractor. That would have meant admitting defeat and so I tried again and then again and after slipping back three times the vehicle finally gained the traction it needed on the fourth attempt and the whole rig moved forwards. I was free. It was now possible to drive out of the undergrowth and onto the woodland path and away back to

Liverpool Road, leaving behind an area of crushed, mangled and demolished foliage of which I never heard another thing.

CLEGG STREET OLDHAM

My plan was to work the required three months and then apply for a transfer from Liverpool road to Freighliner at Longsight But to facilitate this I had to go on loan, for a number of months, to Oldham Road Goods Depot, where they had thirty two tonners with fifth wheel couplings on which one had to prove ones worth by driving one of the managers around the local area with an empty trailer and then uncouple and re-couple the trailer to demonstrate that one had the necessary capabilities. The managers at Oldham Road called those vehicles Hi-Caps, which stood for High Capacity vehicles. The move was OK by me, although unnecessary as I had driven numerous 32 tonners in the time I was away from the railway and was quite adept with those types of vehicle.

I had driven the Hi-Caps for a couple of months when, just before Christmas an offer to work out of Oldham, Clegg Street parcels depot, was given to a number of drivers, including myself, as they had a shortage of drivers and could not cope with the amount of loaded trailers that came from the numerous mail order mills in the area. The offer was accepted by me and a few other drivers who agreed to work at Oldham during the run up to Christmas.

The job entailed driving Scammell Scarab's and Karrier Bantam's running empty trailers or trailers with returned goods to any of the mills, dropping them on a bay and pulling a full one off and returning to Clegg Street where the trailers were usually dropped on the trailer park and an empty picked up for the next trip. The loaded trailers were then taken to the carriages by a shunter and the loads transferred to the trains. The empty trailers would then be dropped on the trailer park. The work was similar to working on the GUS contract at Ardwick, indeed some of the mills were GUS establishments. Others belonged to any of the numerous mail order companies that were operating at the time.

Whereas drivers were brought in from other depots to make up the shortfall, the extra loading staff were employed through various employment agencies and it turned out that a lot of the temporary staff were not to be trusted. Some were opportunist thieves and some, it seems, stole to order. Mail order clientele are usually those that cannot afford to pay cash and so buy on the never-never and are, therefore, those who can least afford to lose their purchases to thieves.

On my first trip I returned to the depot with a trailer that was stacked to the gunwales with mail order parcels for delivery in the North East of the country. The parcels generally were for delivery to private households on council estates and, at that time of the year, were mostly Christmas presents.

Because, at that particular time, there were no empty trailers available on the trailer park I had to pull alongside the train and off-load directly into the carriages. In each carriage that was being loaded were three agency workers stacking the packages for transit. It was then my job to throw the packages from the trailer to the carriage for these men to stack. As they caught the parcels they would throw them on to the stack, slowly filling the carriage.

It became somewhat noticeable that the big parcels were thrown straight onto the stack but the smaller parcels, anything less than approximately nine inches square, were thrown to one side including packages no bigger than one's hand. I thought this a little strange until I noticed one of these agency workers start lifting the small parcels and squeezing and prodding them in an attempt to ascertain what was within. I then saw him tear open the packaging of one of these packets and empty the contents into his hand which swiftly went to his pocket. The open package was then thrown onto the stack and soon became buried beneath more, bigger parcels.

This performance was witnessed a few more times with each of the loaders taking his turn on the little packets, when I felt obligated to ask one of them. 'Excuse me, but what's going on here?'

The response I got was as follows, 'Well mate, we're paid shit wages for pullin' our tripes out, so we're gonna get summat out of it, an' all dese small packets have watches and rings and all other bitsa' jew'll'ry in 'em, small enough to shove in yer pockets to sell int' pub later, so say nowt, or else. D'y'unnerstand?'

'OK mate,' I replied, 'it's nowt to do with me.' But I thought to myself, they're going to get caught soon enough anyway and so I never reported what I had seen. But after talking to other drivers it became patently obvious that it was common knowledge what was going on and it went deeper than I knew.

During the week prior to Christmas in the mid afternoon of a day I returned to the depot from one of the mills and saw numerous police vehicles parked on the approach road to the depot. I drove into the yard and dropped my trailer in the trailer park where I picked up an empty. I then walked over to a porter who was stood by the track and I asked 'What are all those police vehicles doing outside and where is everybody?'

'They came at about dinner time,' he said 'and went to arrest one of the agency men who did a runner, when the others saw what was going on they scattered. Some of 'em shot across the tracks into Glodwick, others went over the wall. Some ran out of the gate and straight into the open arms of the law. They've got about twenty men in the offices now but they're not all agency lads, some of them are railway employees who've been here for years.'

My understanding was that numerous Temporary staff and a few railway employees were prosecuted although I had moved back to Oldham Road and then back to Liverpool Road before the outcome of these cases was known. So what I understood was purely conjecture.

Back at Liverpool Road I was, once again, driving Class 1 vehicles but back on TK Bedford's with the Scammell Automatic Coupling, delivering twelve ton bulk loads locally instead of driving vehicles with the fifth wheel coupling rated at thirty two tons on greater distances, but I knew that within a few weeks my transfer to Freightliner, Longsight would be through, but not before Billy Brougham and I were sent to help out at Halliwell goods depot at Bolton.

The idea was that we would book on at 07.00hrs at Liverpool Road, check our vehicles over and drive to Halliwell Goods yard solo i.e. without a trailer. When at the Bolton Depot we would pull their trailers with our own units and at the end of the day return to Liverpool Road to book off.

Halliwell was a steel depot and all the loads were either sheet steel or bar and girders with the occasional coil of steel. Halliwell depot had a mixed fleet consisting of thirty two tonners equipped with fifth wheel couplings with numerous trombone trailers to which the fifth wheelers could connect and a number of lighter units fitted with the Scammell automatic coupling that could only be used with trailers that were fitted with the Scammell automatic coupling undercarriage.

The majority of the trailers, be they fifth wheel or Scammell, were of the trombone type which, depending on the weight of the load, could be stretched to fifty feet. The longer the trailers were stretched the lower the pay load they could carry. Both Billy and myself were called on to pull these trailers when stretched to their limit and back then in the early seventies, even though we were experienced class one drivers, we found it a little disconcerting pulling our first fifty feet trailers

Whilst at Halliwell we were given all the help and instruction that we needed by the experienced steel men that had worked on this job most of their working lives. Our time at Halliwell was only a couple of weeks but it was a great experience and another string to the bow, so to speak and upon returning to Liverpool Road my transfer to Freightliner was waiting for me.

CHAPTER 12
FREIGHTLINER

Containerisation was, as seems to be universally accepted, the brainchild of British Railways with debts to its sister company Pickfords. Pickfords' started their containerisation by way of custom built, strengthened, wooden crates in which were packed customers goods for delivery. These containers were made to fit the dimensions of road going vehicles and were roped or chained to the flat bed of the delivery vehicle.

British Railways went one better than Pickfords when it introduced its type 'A', 'B' and 'BD' containers in 1928. These containers were of a wooden and steel construction and came in different sizes and many guises, some with doors to the front, some with doors to the rear and some that were constructed to be loaded from the sides and different permutations of all these designs. They differed from earlier styles of container insomuch as they were interchangeable between railway wagons and road vehicles and had loading doors built into them.

These 'A', 'B' and 'BD' types had at each corner and situated about two feet up from the base, anchor points which corresponded to anchor points on the railway wagons or the road vehicles. A three piece tensioning rod with a threaded bar at either end connected to a central, manually operated, threaded, revolving receiver which was turned by means of a toggle bar was employed at each corner to secure these containers to their vehicles, be they road vehicles or rail wagons.

Each threaded bar had a hook at the end. The bars had opposing threads so that when the hooks on them were slotted into the anchor points on the road vehicle or rail wagon and the toggle bar was screwed clockwise, the opposing threads would wind towards one another applying torsion to the whole of the three piece tensioning bar thus securing the container to whichever bed it was sited on. The toggle bars were screwed anti-clockwise to release the containers. The type of restraining bar described above was in use until the ISO twist lock became popular.

Freightliner, before privatisation, was the dedicated, container branch of the British Railways Board (BRB). Its inception was instigated by Dr Beeching, famous for the axing of many rural rail lines during the dramatic reforms he introduced in the 1960's. These reforms led to the formation of the Freightliner Intermodal, whereby British Rail began to move freight using ISO twist lock containers on flat bed wagons between a series of dedicated inland terminals and ports. The containers were transferred from train to road vehicles and vice versa by huge gantry cranes which straddled the rail tracks.

The idea of moving containers filled with goods around the U.K. by rail with final delivery, within a small radius of the terminal, by road is credited to Beeching and is still considered to be the basic premise of Freightliner Intermodal.

Although initially intended for domestic freight alone using its own containers, it soon became the favoured mode of foreign, maritime container movement from deep sea ports such as Southampton Maritime and Felixstowe and inland distribution terminals associated with industry and manufacturing such as Birmingham, Landor Street and Manchester, Trafford Park. It was on 15th November 1965 that the first Freightliner container train ran. It ran from London Kings Cross to Glasgow. Freightliner

Intermodal now has fifteen terminals and moves in excess of five hundred thousand containers per annum.

On 19th of November 1968 Freightliner became a limited company under the 1968 Transport Act with 51% shareholding vested in the National Freight Corporation. In 1976 Freightliner was transferred to the British Rail Board from NFC by the 1976 Transport Act and in 1978 the control of Freightliner transferred entirely to the BRB from NFC by the Transport Act of that year. Finally in 1988 Freightliner was incorporated into Rail Freight Distribution in 1995/6, prior to privatisation.

After operating as part of British Rail and the NFC for over thirty years, Freightliner was privatised as a stand alone company, being bought out by its own management.

In 1999, the new company set up its heavy Haul business alongside its intermodal container operation. The Heavy haul started by moving ballast and rails for the railway infrastructure, later moving into other bulk loads including cement, coal, aggregates and scrap metal.

In 2006 Freightliner expanded it operations into Poland, which since the collapse of communism in 1985 has been established as a liberal democracy. A subsidiary company named Freightliner PL was established to exploit the high volume of coal traffic and the liberalisation of the Polish Railway system.

The newly established company bought seven new 'Class 66' locomotives and four hundred and thirty two new hopper wagons to allow this service to go ahead. This makes Freightliner PL the first private freight operator in Poland to work with completely new rolling stock.

Freightliner, it is said, is in the process of concluding an agreement with a partner in Germany to operate cross border traffic, targeting petroleum and aggregates to add to their movements of coal.

CHAPTER 13
FREIGHTLINER LONGSIGHT

I started work at the Longsight Freightliner Terminal, Manchester early in 1971. The Longsight terminal was situated on New Bank Street adjacent to the Longsight rail sheds and maintenance and cleaning depot and was on a spur from the Piccadilly-Stockport line.

The vehicles at Longsight were a mixture of Guy Big J's, and Seddon 32: Four models, all rated at 32 tons. They were all painted in the railways yellow and some of the older Seddon's were hand me downs from Railfreight. The Seddon 32: Fours; were fibre glass cabbed and were fitted with the Rolls Royce 220, AEC; AV690 or AV760 diesels and the AEC straight six constant mesh gearboxes. These last two engines and gearboxes, when fitted in the Seddon's, were only offered to Freightliner and BRS. The Seddon's were fitted with a ratchet hand brake to the right of the driver's seat. Some had the two piece split windscreen whilst the later models had the one piece screen.

The Guy Big J, which was introduced in 1964 when Jaguar motors bought the Guy Motor Company, had an all steel Motor Panels cab and the J in Big J signified that it was a Jaguar product. The usual engine fitted to these vehicles was the Cummins' V6-200 coupled to a four over four or five over five, Eaton Fuller gearbox although any choice of engine and gearbox could be specified. The engines used back then on 32 ton operation ranged from 150 to 220bhp, nowadays four and six wheelers have bigger and more powerful engines. The trailers employed on container work were twenty, thirty and forty feet skeletal, twist lock trailers.

Longsight, like a number of other Freightliner terminals, was also home to the transport sector of London Brick. The London Brick Company chartered Railways' rolling stock to bring their product, loaded on full trains of flat bed containers, up from their Bedfordshire and Peterborough brick works to be delivered locally by their own fleet of four and six wheelers which were based at and parked within the terminals. After the deliveries had been made the empty flat beds were returned, via the chartered rolling stock, to the relevant brick making facility to be reloaded and turned around.

Longsight was the only Freightliner Terminal in Manchester at the time and would remain so until the new Trafford Park Terminal opened. The two termini then ran in tandem during the transitional period, when eventually Longsight closed and those staff that did not take redundancy or early retirement moved to the new terminal along with personnel from all the other goods depots which were facing an uncertain future and which would ultimately close.

ROUNDABOUTS AND CORNERS

Lane discipline on our roads seems to be something that the average motorist was and still is completely oblivious to, that and the lack of understanding of the way large, long vehicles act and react when cornering or negotiating roundabouts can lead to some rather nasty accidents with the possibility of fatalities. The average car driver, being unaware, through lack of understanding, ignorance or sheer bloody impatience, will try to pass an LGV at the most inappropriate and inopportune moments and while I understand the frustration felt when behind a large slow moving vehicle, common sense should surely prevail.

Whilst working at Longsight Freightliner Terminal an accident almost befell me when I was travelling along the A679 between Blackburn and Burnley. I approached a road junction where I had to make a left turn. The said junction was controlled by traffic lights which were on red as I approached them. I signalled my intention to turn left about fifty yards prior to the junction and because it was a tight corner, considering I was pulling a forty feet trailer, I positioned myself towards the centre of the road so as to avoid mounting the kerb when I made my manoeuvre. My nearside indicator was flashing throughout.

When the traffic lights changed to green in my favour I put my vehicle in gear and released the hand brake. I glanced in my mirrors including the kerbing mirror which is a fixture mounted above the nearside door and angled down towards the kerb. Lo and behold, what did I see? By my side, about a couple of inches from my cab and with the nearside tyres scrubbing the kerb was a mini, obviously containing a very stupid driver.

If I had pulled away and made my manoeuvre the car driver would have had to take evasive action by driving on the pavement or risk being crushed under my trailer which contained a twenty tons load. As it was I let the car pull away. The vehicle did not turn left but was driven into the junction and so, to show my exasperation, I blew my horn at the little Austin and its driver. The little car stopped half way across the junction and the door opened. A young, long haired youth exited the vehicle and started to gesticulate wildly with his arms as he gave me a load of verbal abuse followed by the 'V' sign. He then got back behind the wheel of the mini and drove away. It seemed to me at the time that some drivers had not got the sense they were born with and sadly this is still true today.

Other stupid and inconsiderate drivers are not always quite as lucky as the chap in the mini, as an accident that happened to a driver at Longsight will demonstrate. The driver concerned was called Norman, Little Norman to all the other drivers at the Longsight terminal. Norman, a middle aged man from Oldham, was just five feet, four inches tall and his vehicle was adapted to suit his height. This adaptation was such that the pedals of the vehicle had small blocks fitted to them to ensure that he was able to reach them. This was a ministry approved modification of the vehicle carried out by the Freightliner fitters.

One day, as Norman approached a roundabout, during the course of his working day, he signalled his intention to turn right. Because he was pulling a forty feet trailer and because trailers when cornering or negotiating roundabouts have a tendency to cut in, Norman positioned his vehicle so that the rear end of the trailer would not mount the high Kerb of the roundabout. Like most LGV drivers, he tried to cover every eventuality, constantly checking his mirrors, but apparently some fish slip through the net.

Norman's indicator was flashing his intention throughout the manoeuvre and as the artic and driver negotiated the roundabout the driver of a high powered sports car; a chancer who seemed to have been born with very little sense, attempted to sneak up the inside and past Norman's vehicle. Unfortunately he came terribly unstuck as in Norman's words: 'I looked in my off-side mirror and saw the road was clear. A couple of seconds later I felt a bump and looked again to see the leading axle of my trailer climbing up the boot of a sports car.'

The accident occurred as a result of the driver of the sports car's bad judgement. He had squeezed in between the roundabout Kerb and the rear axles of the trailer, with very little room to spare. He had then realised that the trailer was cutting in on him and, for some reason known only to himself, he decided to stop. He didn't stop and sound his horn; he just stopped and waited for the inevitable collision. If he had blown his horn, Norman may have checked his off side mirror a second earlier and stopped before the impact.

After the impact and an angry exchange the police were called, the road was cleared, statements were taken, witnesses were consulted and the car driver was charged, by the police, with driving without due care and attention. Norman gave his account of what had occurred to the police officers in attendance and they having knowledge of traffic incidents of that kind absolved him of any offence. The case though, did go to court where the same verdict was given.

These types of incidents raise certain questions to the problems of driver awareness, or the lack of, the main question being: Why aren't learner drivers instructed on the behaviour of long articulated or even long rigid vehicles, on the way they act and react on roundabouts and at corners? If the theory of swing out and walk back of large vehicles with long, rear overhangs was taught, prior to the driving test, a lot of heartbreak, injury and perhaps death could be avoided.

³TDI, ROLLS ROYCE AND BONEMEAL

It was while I was working at the Longsight Terminal that a serious accident occurred. This was caused by a supervisor and any number of other personnel, including the engine driver. All concerned parties shall remain nameless to minimise any embarrassment. The accident or incident was basically caused by a lack of liaison between a number of railway staff.

It was early one morning when the signal lights on the exit track were showing green. The train's leaving time had been reached and the supervisor blew the whistle for the train's departure. The train started forward. Unfortunately the straddle

---

3. A fuller and more in depth account of this incident can be found in the earlier book 'This Truckin' Life.'

crane was in the process of depositing a container between two already sited containers on one of the carriages. As the train inched forward it pulled the crane along for a few feet and then the crane began to topple forwards. It crashed down onto the slowly moving, laden train landing on the containers already on the train. The container that the crane was carrying was a tank container full of toluene di-isocyanate (TDI) which was badly damaged and ruptured, another damaged container held two Rolls Royce vehicles which were badly damaged and yet a third container that was burst open contained bonemeal.

The train was immediately brought to a halt. The crane driver climbed out of the wreckage and dusted himself down; he was found to be suffering only from shock and a few cuts and bruises although he was made to attend hospital for a check over. An ambulance was called along with the fire brigade and the police. Phone lines were red hot as calls were made to the emergency numbers on the hazard cards found on the containers. Rolls Royce was contacted and heavy lifting gear was sent for. The Health and Safety Executive were contacted and they sent out their Inspector for Railways and a major enquiry began.

Toluene Di-isocyanate is a chemical compound used in the plastics and motor industries one of its uses is for the hardening of foam for car seats to make the foam rigid. It is a very dangerous substance calling for breathing apparatus to be worn when discharging. If breathed in it crystallises on the lungs and causes lung collapse and it is also carcinogenic and highly toxic.

The tanks that TDI arrived in, once lifted from the train and placed onto a trailer, had to be plugged into an electrical point. The tanks were insulated and had thermo coils built into them. After an overnight journey by train the TDI would have cooled down and solidified, hence the need to connect them to an electrical supply to heat it up and liquefy it once more. The tank would have only been unconnected from the electrical supply immediately prior to its road journey to its delivery point.

Because of the adverse affects of the TDI, all the houses on New Bank Street, opposite the terminal, had to be evacuated until the liquid had been contained and that which had escaped made safe. Only then, when the emergency services and the experts that were called in had declared the area safe, were the residents that had been evacuated allowed back to their homes.

The two Rolls Royce's that were in a forty feet container suffered extensive damage. Rolls Royce investigators were sent to Longsight to assess the damage and to put sheets over the vehicles to stop the press photographers from taking pictures of them. The Rolls Royce staff, however, were too late to stop the disappearance of the Spirit of Ecstasy Statuettes from the radiators. Rumour has it that the only people that could have taken these highly collectable items were the fitters or mechanics from the terminal because it was thought that they were the only people with the tools to liberate the two flying ladies.

The container of bonemeal that was burst open started a small scale anthrax scare until the specialists, dressed in white overalls, that were called in declared it safe. While all the chaos was going on all the staff were told to stay within the confines of the canteen/mess room.

After the official enquiries, one by the HSE and an internal inquiry by the Railway's Board, it seemed that someone's head would roll and severe disciplinary measures would be taken. I don't know whether a scapegoat was offered up on the sacrificial altar but nobody actually lost their jobs over the incident and after a while things returned to a semblance of normality.

AN INTERDEPARTMENTAL MOVE

It wasn't long before I got itchy feet and the urge to move to try something new. I had come to the conclusion that a change was needed. The Railways published a vacancy list every couple of weeks which gave notice of any and all vacancies nationally and included all the railway's associated companies. Under the section for drivers I found a vacancy for a class one driver at the Woolworth's distribution depot at NCL in Castleton, Rochdale. An application was tendered by me for the job and an interview offered some two weeks later.

I was interviewed at the Castleton depot by the traffic foreman, Alan Walsh, who had been the foreman at Oldham Clegg Street when I worked there for the Christmas rush a couple of years earlier. He remembered me and was suitably impressed. The post was offered to me and I accepted and was given a starting date and duly moved over to the Woolworth's contract. Because this was an interdepartmental move there was no loss of perks, privileges or seniority.

The job entailed, as one might imagine, delivering to Woolworth's stores all over this little nation of ours, but there was also another side to this job. That other side was the collection from all of Woolworth's suppliers with goods that were delivered back to the distribution depot or other NCL depots nationwide. Now I've never been a keen shop delivery man and my plan was to get on the supplies side of the job and to do that I had to use what little seniority I had. I only did a few weeks on shop deliveries before I secured a post on the supplies side. Like the shop deliveries this meant that one might be out all week but between two and four nights out was the norm although one could be stuck on locals for weeks on end on shop deliveries. Conversely one could be on shop deliveries in Scotland and when empty be directed to a suppliers warehouse to pick up a load for Castleton.

Some of the delivery points for the stores were in some of the most inaccessible places. One I remember as being probably the worst store in the country for accepting deliveries was the Warrington store. The delivery bay was down a side street in the centre of the town. Cars were parked on either side of the road and the delivery bay was from the days of the horse and cart. Manoeuvrability was so bad that only twenty foot trailers could be used and once backed in the unit still protruded into the carriageway. This of course caused pedestrians to walk in the road, a dangerous pastime. Drivers delivering to this store were always being threatened by traffic wardens or law enforcement officers. These threats were for the offence of causing an obstruction on the Queen's highway. I don't know whether the problems at this store were ever resolved.

Some of the smaller Woolworth's stores did not have a delivery point at the rear of the store and deliveries had to be made through the front door. This, at times, meant parking partly on the pavement to allow the free flow of traffic. A lot of these stores had double yellow lines outside and once again this led to confrontation between the driver and law enforcement officers. Generally, shop deliveries, at stores such as Woolworth's and other big multi nationals, are a pain in the arse for the driver, due to parking restrictions, traffic wardens, the general public, lack of room and a whole host of other problems.

On the supplies side many and varied loads were carried. The trailer on one occasion might be filled from back to front and from ceiling to floor with jigsaw puzzles and then the next load might be a full load of ladies lingerie or any other commodity that Woolworth's sold in their stores. At other times two collections might be loaded into the same trailer resulting in a split load from two suppliers.

A lot of these manufacturers, especially the toy manufacturers, would give the driver a sample of their goods. Whether this was given as a bribe to stop the driver stealing from the load or whether it was given from the goodness of the manufacturer's heart I don't know, but my young daughters became very adept at jigsaw puzzles and had countless different types of dolls and other toys to play with, thanks to the kindness of the manufacturers of Woolworth's supplies.

SHOPPER'S WORLD

On the Woolworth's contract there was a couple of four wheelers used to service speciality shops that belonged to Woolworth's. These shops were known as Shopper's World and were run on a similar basis to the way Argos is run today. All the goods to be delivered to Shopper's World were packed into wheeled cages which were rolled into the rear of the vehicle which was fitted with a tail lift. The full cages were left at the store. The empty cages and any returns were picked up when the next delivery was made.

On the London run to Shopper's World there was employed a black guy who did two runs a week to the London shop which was to be found on Kensington High Street near to Holland's Walk where the mews which housed the royal stables was once situated. The job was a guaranteed two nights out, but it was common knowledge amongst the drivers that Charlie, the black guy, did it there and back in the day. He booked off somewhere around Stafford or Wolverhampton and ran home off the book or bent, as it was termed. This ensured that he spent more time with his family and made a few extra pounds on the subsistence money.

One Monday he phoned in sick and said he would be off for the week. I had not been allocated a job that day so the two London runs fell to me.

Because I was late setting off I experienced problems with traffic flow falling foul of rush hour traffic at Birmingham etc; I arrived at my destination late and had to wait to be unloaded. By the time I was unloaded and reloaded I realised that I was not going to get far that evening so I ran the short distance to Paddington Station where I had decided I would spend the night. I had a word with the driver's foreman and was told that I could avail myself of the mess room as a bedroom for the night, instead of sleeping in the cab.

Having a few hours to kill before bed time I decided that I would have a ride out to Stoke Newington to see my aunt and my uncle who lived in that hamlet. Being the days before the dreaded tachograph was implemented and imposed upon the haulage industry; I used the delivery vehicle to drive down the A501 Marylebone Road, Euston Road, Pentonville and City Road to the A10, Kingsland Road and so up to Stoke Newington which is off the main Cambridge road.

I had not seen my aunt Lou, my father's sister or her Husband Bill Bellini for 15 years or so, but upon seeing me, stood before her on the doorstep, she recognised me immediately and shouted to my uncle, 'Bill, Come see who's here, it's our boy's boy.'

My father was known as boy because in his days as a boxer, in the RAF; he fought under the name of Boy Pepper. Pepper being his mother's maiden name.

I was invited in, fed and watered and had a couple of beers with my uncle Bill. We caught up on old times and before I knew it, it was time to go. My aunt Lou offered to make me up a bed for the night but I politely refused, saying that I already had digs. Really, I did not wish to impose myself upon their good nature and hospitality and so returned to Paddington Station where I parked up. I then carried my sleeping bag to the mess room, performed my evening ablutions and prostrated myself along a padded bench seat close to the fire. Pleasantly ensconced within my sleeping bag I fell soundly asleep and did not awaken until the early shift came on at 0600 hrs; the next morning.

As the station staff arrived for duty I deemed it polite to rise and perform my morning lavation. My functions taken care of, I returned to the mess where a cup of tea was proffered by the early shift. This I gratefully accepted before going out into the yard and checking my wagon over prior to leaving Paddington to set off for Manchester at a leisurely pace. I pulled off the M1 at junction nine for the A5 and called into the Watling Street Café for breakfast.

After my morning repast I climbed back into my vehicle and drove out of the café lorry park onto the A5 and rejoined the motorway. Being in no rush I trundled along and arrived back in the Woolworth's depot at Castleton five hours later where I tipped and reloaded for my next trip to London on the Wednesday.

On my second trip I got away to an early start and because the vehicle that I was using at that time was capable of seventy plus mph; my journey time from Manchester to Kensington High Street was just four and a half hours. The unloading and reloading was attended to immediately upon my arrival and took less than an hour to complete. The prompt service that I received at the London store enabled me to get a bite to eat before I proceeded on my return journey. I arrived back in Manchester and parked up outside my house at 1730hrs.

That night was spent with my wife in my own bed and we enjoyed a lie in the next morning and to top it all off I was better off to the tune of a night's subsistence money. It is pertinent to stress that speeding at up to seventy mph; was not the norm for a driver employed within the railways' group of companies. A driver would only drive at this speed if there was something in it for himself, as in the case described whereby I profited to the tune of my night out money and the comforts of home and wife.

The 'there and back in a day' fiddle came to an end when Charlie had an accident as he turned into the street on which he lived while he was on a dodgy night out. He had already filled in his log book which showed that he was in Cheslyn Hay near Cannock.

The accident in which Charlie was involved was caused when he ran into the rear of a car which had suddenly stopped. It was his fault and besides having to make an accident report out he had to explain why he was outside his home when he should have been parked up somewhere around the Midlands area. His excuse was that he had received information that his wife had been taken ill and he thought that the best thing to do was to get home to be by her side. Sadly it was just an excuse and it was seen through by the gaffer. He promptly offered back to the company the night out money which he had drawn. For his troubles Charlie received a severe disciplinary warning and was demoted to local runs for a time. He actually got off light for what was a sackable offence with elements of fraud and embezzlement.

A RUDE AWAKENING

When nighted out the drivers on the Woolworth's contract would sometimes cab it, i.e. sleep in the cab on a makeshift bed, with makeshift curtains on a wire around the interior of the cab. That was because all the vehicles of the day were day cabs and were not fitted with bunks. Those nights out when sleeping in the cab would normally be spent in railway yards which were now given over to NCL (National Carriers Limited).

The object of this exercise was to make some extra money so about half of the nights out were spent in the cab and the other half in digs. Of course this ratio changed in the winter months when, because there were no night heaters in the cabs, more nights were spent in digs.

It was on a mid week's summer's night that I and another driver, by the name of John Williams, decided that we would cab it in the railway/NCL yard on London Road, Carlisle. We made up our beds before going for our evening meal which was followed by a few pints. Those makeshift beds consisted of a board lay across the engine cover and balanced on the window ledge in the door, with a sleeping bag laid along its length. The driver's overnight case would be placed on one of the seats to bring it level with the engine cover and to offer a little support. One could still enter and exit the cab because there was no weight on the board and so the doors could be opened without the board moving.

We washed in the depot toilets and got changed into clean clothes and went to satisfy our hunger and our thirst. We returned to our vehicles at about 2230 hours. We entered our respective cabs and after closing the makeshift curtains, (usually run up by wives or girlfriends) the acrobatics of getting ready for bed in such a confined space began. Finally one would wriggle into the warmth of the sleeping bag and wait for the arms of Morpheus to embrace one.

Next morning, at approximately 0630, I was aroused by noise and movement in the yard and so I threw my blankets back, and got dressed and stowed away my bed and the curtains behind the seats. I then gathered my washing tackle, tooth brush etc; together and exited the cab. I walked round to John's cab and without thinking I grabbed the door handle and pulled. Surprisingly, John had not locked the door, either forgetting, due to alcohol intake, or probably thinking it was not necessary within the confines and sanctity of the NCL yard.

As the door sprang open I noticed fleetingly that John was fast asleep, still incarcerated in his sleeping bag which had slipped off the window ledge as I opened the door. The bed tilted and slid out of the opening with John still cocooned in the bag which had a Union Jack design on it. It was like watching a burial at sea as the board and its contents left the cab at about forty five degrees and hit the ground almost vertical. The bed crashed to the floor and John got the rudest awakening of his life. I have never seen anybody extricate themselves from a sleeping bag quite as sharply as John did that morning. Amidst the swearing and cursing, he was dancing and prancing around the yard dressed only in his underpants and vest. Not a pretty sight.

Apologies came very hard as I was doubled up with laughter and could barely speak. John was shaken but unhurt, although a few contusions did become noticeable some time later. He calmed down and climbed back into his cab to get dressed. As he did so I gathered up his bed and bedding and by the time we were making our way to the toilets he began to see the funny side of the incident and was even laughing about it himself.

We left the NCL yard at about 0715hrs and drove up to Crawford on the old A74 where we had breakfast at the Heatherghyll Truck Stop. After breakfast we parted company. My route was along the A702 towards Edinburgh and John carried on up the A74 towards Glasgow. We would not meet again until the week-end.

HAVE A PHEASANT JOURNEY

It was whilst on another trip to Scotland when a singularly odd thing happened, as odd things do, that is when they are least expected. I was on my way to Edinburgh and had turned off the A74 and once again onto the A702 heading towards Biggar in a North Easterly direction. Radio 2 was belting out and my concentration was on the road ahead with occasional glances into the rear view mirrors to watch out for the ubiquitous Scottish law enforcement officers. Suddenly there was a sudden burst of sound, a loud, ear splitting report and I was showered with broken glass. The surprise and shock of the sudden crash very near gave me a heart attack and I glanced over to whence the noise had emanated and found myself looking through an unglazed hole where my near side door window used to be. I then glanced down to the passenger seat to see a large pheasant, strewn with glass and in its death throes.

This long tailed, brightly coloured, but stupid bird had flown into and through my near side door window and crash-landed onto the passenger seat.

The vehicle was brought to a halt and I alighted from my cab and walked around to the passenger side and opened the door. The pheasant, by that time, had shuffled off its avian coil. It lay there, in all its colourful glory, with a look of serenity in its still open eyes. Carefully I lifted the corpse of the deceased game bird and as I did so it flopped over my arm as if every bone in its body was broken, as every bone in its body probably was. Strangely there was no bleeding from the cadaver of the once vivacious bird, even after it had committed Hara-Kiri via Kamikaze through the window of my cab.

There was very little that I could do, the last rites over dead fowl is not in my remit, so I threw it, unceremoniously into the hedgerow for the carrion to dispose of. The next duty I had to perform was to find a public telephone and call my home depot to report what had occurred. I drove for a couple of miles and just outside Biggar I found the telephone kiosk for which I searched. I made the requisite call and the home depot arranged for a local vehicle window replacement company to come out and repair the damage. Once this was accomplished I carried on with the job, albeit, somewhat later than expected.

CHAPTER 14
FREIGHTLINER, TRAFFORD PARK

In 1971 the new Freightliner Terminal opened in Trafford Park at about the same time that the Containerbase on Barton Dock Road opened for business and within a year the Longsight Terminal closed. Because the Containerbase dealt with maritime containers most of the employees were ex Dockers from the recently partially closed Manchester docks. The docks suffered full closure in 1982.

The Trafford Park Freightliner Terminal was built on the land that had housed the Trafford Park loco sheds which were demolished in 1969 to make way for the new terminal which opened in 1971.

The staff that made up the Trafford Park Freighliner workforce was from Deansgate and Victoria Parcels Depots and all the many and various goods depots that were closing, plus those Freightliner drivers from the Longsight Terminal that did not take early retirement or redundancy. Other drivers had been employed on the Speedfreight network which was included in the 1963 timetable following year long trials. Speedfreight was the forerunner of Freightliner.

The drivers that came from Deansgate and Victoria and probably from other local rail depots were rushed through their HGV tests to fill the vacancies that existed at Freightliner Trafford Park. The railway's, at that time, preferred to employ people that had a railway background and because a lot of the old goods yards were due to close, it made perfect sense to enable those employees that wished to take up the option to do so.

I saw a new opportunity and applied, by way of the interdepartmental vacancy list, for a post of Class1 driver at Trafford Park and early in 1973 I left the Woolworth's contract and I once again became a Freightliner driver. I knew all the guys that came from Deansgate, Victoria and Oldham Road, they are mentioned earlier. Those that came from Longsight Freightliner Terminal were: Ernie Beswick, George Robertson, Walter Harrabin, Len Hodgkinson, Noel Smith and Jack Harrison and one or two others whose names now elude me.

Luckily, when they closed the Longsight Terminal the old vehicles that were the Longsight fleet were deemed not fit for purpose and were scrapped. The vehicles that were at Trafford Park, however, were not much better and included the Seddon 34:4, powered by the AEC, AV 691 engine with a David Brown straight six transmission. Later a number of Leyland Marathon's with the 265 Rolls Royce engine mated to an Eaton Fullers four over four gearbox and a number of Guy Big J's with the 200 Cummin's and Fuller's range change. A number of Ergomatic cabbed AEC Mandator's were brought into the fleet, these were fitted with an AEC engine with a straight six gearbox or the Eaton Fuller option.

The most unusual vehicle to be introduced to the Freightliner Fleet at the time was the Volvo F86. Unusual because being a nationalised company the policy was to buy British trucks. However, because British vehicle manufacturers were in a massive downward spiral of decline and because the Swedish marque was actually built at a plant in Irvine in Scotland it was deemed that these Volvo's were part British and the Scottish plant kept a large number of Scottish people in gainful employment and off the dole.

Most of the containers that came into the Manchester terminal were destined to go no further than limits of Trafford Park, others would travel no further than the boundaries of Manchester and yet others would go no further than the Lancashire, Cheshire and Staffordshire borders. Sometimes their would be deliveries into Cumbria, Northumbria and even into North Wales and occasionally into South Wales, but mainly the trips that were done were usually of the type that could be done in the working day without transgressing the drivers hours rules.

Some of the older drivers were quite happy to just poodle around the town, mainly because that was what they were used to doing before Freightliner came into being.

There was one driver named Harry Taylor who did nothing but run Manchester Liner's containers into Vere Street on the docks, and bring other Manchester Liner's containers back to the terminal. Harry's vehicle could regularly be seen parked outside the Broadway pub, a Holt's beer house, on Broadway, Salford close to the docks. Another couple of drivers did nothing else but run back and forth between the terminal and the Containerbase.

Like all new starters at Trafford Park I was sent out with another driver for assessment of my driving capabilities, although I found this a bit stupid as I had passed my original driving test with the railways and had my domestic license plus experience on a multitude of vehicles. The railway's domestic licence no longer applied and it was then considered enough to assess a driver on any thirty two ton, gross weight vehicle.

The driver I was sent out with was a guy of my own age called John Pardoe. John later transferred to the NCL depot on Preston Street in West Gorton to work on the Newsflow contract and became very active within the NUR (National Union of Railwaymen) which later became the RMT (The National Union of Rail, Maritime and Transport Workers). John, sadly, is no longer with us, but we had a good day together on that assessment, although I missed a gear or two when I thought that I was being scrutinised, nerves I suppose, but I soon got over that. John informed the head of transport, at the terminal, that I was quite competent of driving to the standards required by Freightliner.

The next day, upon reporting for duty, I was informed that there was not a vehicle available for me to drive. The vehicle allocated to me was still in the workshop being serviced. An older ex Speedfreight driver by the name of Harry Lord asked the transport clerk if I might join him as he had a forty feet domestic container to load at a company in Darwen, Lancs that traded under the name of Evertaut. Evertaut were the producers of stackable furniture, the type used in schools and conference rooms where the seating and tables had to be stacked away when not in use. The furniture was made of welded tube with plywood tabletops and seats.

Because the job was all hand ball and would have taken a single person up to four hours to load I was allowed to accompany Harry on that job. As we approached the vehicle that Harry normally drove he walked to the near side and opened the door and seated himself quite comfortably in the passenger seat. I looked at him and he looked at me, then he said 'Well, there's no point in havin' a dog an' barkin' yourself, is there?' So I became the driver for the day.

After picking up an empty forty feet container me and Harry made our way to the Darwen factory of Evertaut. We had a pleasant journey even though it was a cold and frosty morning. We stopped at a roadside catering caravan for a cup of tea and a bacon sarney on the way. The Evertaut factory was just off the A666, Blackburn Road in Darwen and the entrance was off the main road down a fairly steep decline with a dog-leg bend on the driver's blind side to be negotiated. This road down to the loading bay was also iced over.

Upon reaching the site Harry said, 'Right, let's see how good you are.'

To which I responded 'No problem.'

With that Harry alighted from the cab to hold the traffic whilst I reversed off the main road and onto the entrance road down to the loading bay. Harry then went to the rear of the vehicle to watch me back as I negotiated the blind bend. I was reversing at tick over to help prevent any loss of traction on the ice. As I rounded the blind bend with the loading bay now directly behind me I applied the required lock on the steering to bring the prime mover in line with the trailer. Just before the road way levelled off at the bottom of the decline I felt the trailer start to slide. Harry shouted 'WHOOOA! HOLD IT! STOP!'

But there was nothing I could do and the whole rig slid gracefully backwards in a perfectly straight line. It then hit the rubber buffers on the loading bay and stopped in perfect alignment and perfectly centred on the bay. I couldn't have done it any better if I had have been in proper control. Harry appeared at the side of the cab and was about to speak when I lowered the window and said, 'Right, now you've seen how good I am. Not bad, hey?'

By the time we had loaded the container, which took us almost three hours, and we were ready to make the return journey to Trafford Park, the ice on the approach road had melted. I signed for the consignment and closed and sealed the doors and we set off with Harry muttering, 'I ain't ever seen anything like it. Lucky bastard.'

MISHAPS AND MISADVENTURES

Professional truck drivers are usually very good at what they do but occasionally mistakes are made. Driver Walter Harrabin was sent to pick up one of Freightliner's own empty twenty foot boxes from a local company. For this job he had to take an empty twenty foot trailer upon which the container would be deposited by a crane or large fork lift truck and returned to the terminal. Walter hooked up to a four in line trailer.

Four in line trailers had the rear axle set right back to the rear of the trailer and had four equally spaced wheels in line along this axle and they were notoriously unstable, unless designed as a low loader.

Because of the way axle was sited and because of the wheel configuration drivers had to take greater care when cornering as the four in line trailers with their rear set axle needed more room than normal trailers with tandem axles or single axles with a rear overhang. The unaware driver could quite easily mount kerbs and damage street furniture. Walter arrived at the yard where the container was situated, which was in the Stretford area and the box was lifted onto the trailer.

Walter went into the company office to sort out any paperwork. When he came out he went straight to his cab and drove away not realising that the twist locks had been left in the open position.

Whether Walter was in a rush or not cannot be determined but as he was turning left off Chester Road into Trafford Road his nearside rear wheel mounted the kerb and crashed back onto the camber. The sudden drop caused the unsecured container to bounce off the twist locks and tumble sideways over the barrier at the side of the road and onto the pavement, where it landed on its side. Luckily there was nobody walking along this stretch of pavement at the time.

Walter, that day, was extremely fortunate because directly behind him was one of Kaye Goodfellow's heavy cranes, the driver of which stopped to give assistance. Between the crane driver and Walter and for a price, cones were placed in position, the outriggers of the crane were extended and dropped, chains were employed and within ten minutes the container was back on the trailer and the twist locks turned to the locked position. A small crowd had gathered to watch but they dispersed once the operation was completed. Walter thanked the crane driver and gave him a fiver and they departed before any police arrived. The barrier on the corner was flattened and remained so for about three weeks when the council workmen arrived and put things right. The incident was never reported and so no claims were issued. The Trafford Council had to do the repairs of the barrier at their own costs.

Another incident that occurred with a four in line concerned a driver at Trafford Park, although I cannot remember who it was driving at that time. He had mounted the kerb with a thirty feet model of this type of trailer which at the time was carrying a loaded, thirty feet container. At a certain corner as the rear end of the trailer mounted the kerb the container came into contact with the lamp post and was the cause of the street light being pushed over to an angle of forty five degrees. Once again, as luck would have it, there happened to be no pedestrians passing directly by at the time. Although there were people in the vicinity who saw what happened and reported the incident. This resulted in a claim being forwarded to Freightliner and of course the driver had to fill in an accident report for insurance purposes.

Low bridges were sometimes a problem and besides Joe O'Heeney getting stuck under an arched bridge in Penistone when he moved from the centre of the road into the inside lane to allow a car to come the opposite way and thus becoming firmly wedged, there were other incidents.

Jack Harrison, when on a delivery which took him past his house via a small diversion, called in to pick his daughter up. It was the school holidays and Jack had promised his girl that he would take her for a ride out, even though this was frowned upon by the company and any passengers would not be insured.

The delivery which Jack was to do on that day was to a haulage Company in Carnforth, just off the A6. Unfortunately Jack missed the turning for the company and went straight forward and collided with a low, arched railway bridge. Ironically one of the haulage company's employees was waiting at the corner to direct Jack in but Jack did not see the man waving his arms and gesticulating to catch his attention.

On impact with the bridge Jack was thrown through the windscreen and broke his arm. His daughter managed to stay within the cab and suffered lacerations and contusions. The vehicle and its occupants were recovered and taken to different venues for repair. I think Jack received a severe disciplinary warning but it cured him of taking his daughter for a ride out and ultimately he could have faced the sack.

Another incident occurred when I was delivering a load, in a forty feet container to a company in the Yorkshire area, somewhere around the town of Heckmondwyke, if my memory serves me correctly. Following directions I had been given I took a turn into a narrow lane and drove down it for about two miles when I came upon a low railway bridge. There had been no visible signs telling of this bridge as I entered the lane. The bridge was only twelve feet six inches high and my vehicles height was thirteen feet six inches. It occurred to me that a slight problem faced me. I could not turn around due to the narrowness of the road and so the only answer was to get out and direct, around my vehicle, the traffic that had pulled up behind me. That done I proceeded to reverse back down the lane around curves and bends for about three quarters of a mile before I came to a side road that I could reverse into and so enable me to turn around. That was no easy task as I had to reverse across the opposite lane and vehicles were approaching my truck from both directions and I had to make numerous stops to allow them to pass in safety.

When I finally turned around and made my way to the end of that country lane I looked to my left and spotted the sign for the low bridge, almost completely covered by foliage. If the local highway's authority had done their job by cutting back the growth around the sign, it would have saved me, and probably numerous other drivers, a major problem. It had become obvious to me that the narrow lane I had foolishly turned down was the wrong one and that the directions that I had been given stipulated the next major turning. I finally got back on track and delivered the load to its destination a little later than expected.

A week or so later I was going to North Wales with a delivery in a thirty feet maritime container. I was proceeding along Chester Road (A556), at a place where it was only single carriageway, when I noticed, through my rear view mirrors, a vehicle to my rear. The driver of that vehicle was flashing his headlamps continually at me. Thinking that there may be something amiss, I pulled in at the next lay by to check the rear of my truck and as I alighted from my cab the vehicle that had been flashing me sped by at about seventy plus mph. The vehicle was a Range Rover towing a caravan. As it passed I noticed the driver gesturing at me via a masturbatory motion with his hand. It was then that I realised that there was probably nothing wrong with my vehicle. I had just been driving to slow for the impatient idiot who seemed to think he was in the Calgary stampede or the Californian gold rush of 1848 and was possessed of a death wish.

While I was out of my cab I gave my vehicle a cursory once over just to be sure, I then climbed back into the vehicle and set off again. I had only gone another three or four miles when I came upon a queue of standing traffic. The standing traffic started to move slowly forward. After about a hundred yards, at a bend in the road, I came upon the cause of the slow moving traffic. There, to the right, after crossing the oncoming carriageway, was the badly smashed Range Rover on its side. Still connected to the Range Rover was the badly twisted chassis of the caravan which had exploded into a thousand pieces as it capsized. The whole twisted rig was partly on the pavement, partly on the grass verge and slightly touching the carriageway. The road itself was strewn with the debris of what was left of the upper bodywork of the caravan and the driver's personal belongings.

As I drew level with the vehicle and its driver he gazed up at me, his face was streaked with blood, grime and tears. I, at first, was going to return his masturbatory gesture but I didn't have the heart. It seemed to me, that because of his aggressive driving and stupidity, he had enough problems to deal with but I thought: 'Who's the wanker now?' As I weaved my way through, past and over the numerous bits and pieces of wreckage I heard the sirens of the emergency services arriving.

It does seem a little curious that a driver that has had no prior experience at towing can go out and buy a twenty five feet long caravan and drag it down the road. A lot of the time all that is needed is a little common sense but it seems that with some drivers this is sadly lacking. A towing course should be compulsory. Whether the driver in this little tale had any experience or not is not known but if he was experienced he was also very foolish.

There existed, in Blackburn, a steel stockholder to whom I was once sent to load a twenty foot coil carrier, tilt container. Tilt containers come in various guises and different sizes. They are usually twenty or forty feet long. Tilt containers like tilt trailers are soft sided with a hard roof or may have a one piece, totally detachable cover which covers both the sides and the top. The curtains which constitute the sides and/or roof are made of weatherproofed canvas which can be stripped off and folded or drawn back along the framework of the trailer.

When I arrived at the stockholder and I had driven into the concrete floored unloading area, I was told that I would have to perform a complete strip down of the container. I began by undoing all the laces and strapping that held the tilt cover in place. I then tied a rope to the two rear corners and pulled the whole tilt cover towards the front of the container. It was then possible for the overhead crane to deposit the single steel coil, which weighed in excess of fifteen tons, into the specially constructed groove in the floor of the container, built in so that the coil could not move in transit. This depression in the floor of the trailer had, laid across it, planks of wood which would enable the trailer to be used for general cargo as well as steel coils, these had to be removed before the coil was put in place.

I climbed into the rear of the stripped down container to remove the planking and so as to be able to guide the coil into the depression in the floor. I really should not have been in the back of the container due to the fact that it was a maritime box and I was, therefore, uninsured, but it appeared that the stockholder was short staffed that day. So onto the back of the trailer I climbed.

Once the coil was in place on the floor of the container and the loading staff had departed, I had to get down to floor level from the rear of the container by way of the rear doors. Being not very high I decided to jump down. As I jumped, one of the catches which accommodates the custom locks of the container doors and which are situated just below the container floor level on the exterior of the box, caught in the hem at the bottom of my trouser leg. The next thing that I knew was that I was plummeting forwards, head first. As I fell forward the catch pulled my trouser leg up to my shin. I fell rapidly and I put my arms out in front of me in an attempt to break my fall and hopefully without breaking anything else. The palms of my hands broke my fall but due to the rapid speed at which I fell my forehead came into contact with the concrete floor quite hard causing some slight abrasions and a lump the size of an egg.

I was dangling like an upside down string operated marionette, my hands barely scraping the floor and unable to gain any purchase. Embarrassing as I found it, necessity forced me to shout for help. Two of the loading staff heard my cries and rushed to my assistance. Their rush came to a halt when they saw my predicament and stifling their laughter they unhooked me, lowered me to the floor and helped me to my feet. Besides the egg on my forehead, it seems that I had egg on my face. Both my shins were scraped and I had grazes on my hands.

I was given basic first aid at the company's medical centre, made to fill in the accident book and after strapping down the coil and reassembling the tilt was sent on my way. Back at the Freightliner Terminal the bump on my head gave my fellow staff reason to whisper, point and ultimately giggle at my appearance. The giggling turned to loud laughter when the circumstances of my little mishap were made known.

NOT MY JOB

Drivers making deliveries or collections using maritime containers are not allowed to get into the container. This is because the driver is not insured and if an accident should befall that driver he has no redress. This causes problems when a driver is asked to give a hand with the loading or unloading of a maritime container and he refuses. The customer has a tendency to think that the driver is just a lazy bastard despite any explanations given. Of course if a customer were to offer an inducement, then a driver would maybe forget about being uninsured. This, of course, was a matter for the driver and his conscience.

Whilst working out of Trafford Park Freightliner Terminal on a cold, day in the middle of winter, after a heavy downfall of snow, I was told to load two twenty feet containers back to back on a forty feet trailer for transfer to a footwear warehouse in Bradford for early afternoon delivery. Upon arriving at the warehouse, which was located in a yard with a number of other companies. I was instructed by the foreman of the shoe warehouse to jack-knife the trailer onto the unloading bay doors to allow access to the front container. I did as requested and I then broke the seals on the doors and opened up the container and retired back to my cab. I had just made myself a brew when there was a knock upon my cab door. I wound down the window to be greeted by the warehouse foreman. 'Good morning.' he said.

'Good morning to you.' I replied.

'We're ready for you now.' He said, 'You throw the cartons down to my boys and they will stack them away.'

'I'm very sorry,' I said 'but it's more than my job's worth to get in the back of a maritime container. I'm not insured so it's not my job.'

There was a bit of discussion about the fact that I disputed who's responsibility it was to unload and the lack of insurance for the driver and the fact that the goods were his and not mine and then the foreman said, 'Railway workers, you've always been a shower of lazy bastards.' Then he stormed off a little annoyed with me.

After about an hour or so had passed, one of the work staff appeared at the cab to inform me that the front container had been unloaded. I then had to close the doors and reverse away from the loading bay, turn around and reverse back towards the loading bay so that the load within the rear container could be transferred from container to warehouse.

While the front container was being unloaded more snow had fallen and I experienced a lot of wheel spin and traction problems as I attempted to reverse up the slight slope from the loading bay. Eventually I managed to get the trailer into position for the unloading of the rear container, but not without a lot of slipping and sliding on the snow and ice.

I once again got out of my cab to break the seals on the container and open the doors. As I was pinning the doors back the foreman came along and said to me, 'Right, my lads have done the front container without your assistance. So, are you going to give them a hand with this one?'

'I'm sorry mate, I've already told you, I can't do it, it's not my job.'

By the time the second container was empty and I had my paperwork signed and I had closed the container doors it was the warehouse's finishing time. I got into my cab and attempted to pull away. Because there was now no weight in the trailer I had very little traction and it became a struggle to pull away from the warehouse doors; my vehicle would not pull up the slippery incline away from the loading bay. I tried using the diff lock but all this achieved was to get both drive wheels spinning in unison.

As I struggled on the incline, to move my vehicle, the warehouse personnel were vacating the premises and were walking past my vehicle. I opened my window just as the foreman was passing and I asked, 'Is there any chance of getting me some sand or rock salt to put under my wheels?'

He smiled broadly and replied, 'Sorry mate, it's not my job.' Then he walked away with the rest of his staff.

Near to the warehouse doors was a part roll of mesh fencing. The perimeter fence had been renewed and this roll was what was left when the job was finished. Being in the predicament that

I was I unrolled this wire mesh and jammed it under my drive axle and laid it along the ground up the incline. I got back into the cab, started the engine, engaged the differential lock, put the vehicle in gear, applied some revs, released the hand brake and attempted to pull forward. This time the tires bit on the wire mesh and I moved slowly forwards up the incline and out of the yard.

The fencing was ruined but I thought 'Fuck it.' I then realised that I would have to reconsider what answer I should give when asked to help to unload in situations like that in future, although once I had extricated myself from the compacted snow and out of the yard I had to smile at the foreman's response to my plea for help.

CLASS ONE DRIVING. IT'S A PIECE OF CAKE. ISN'T IT?

At a different time during the 1970's, another winter's tale took place whilst working out of Trafford Park Freightliner Terminal; It was a very harsh winter of which I relate when another driver and myself were each given loads to deliver to Stubbins' Paper Mills in Stubbins, Ramsbottom near Bury. The loads consisted of twenty tons of wood pulp for paper making. The other driver, Richard Wilson, Dick to his friends and workmates, found his load to be in a thirty feet 'M' type container. The 'M' type is a curtain sided container similar in construction to the loading area of a Tautliner trailer. My load was on a roped and sheeted, thirty feet flat bed container.

The flat bed containers used by Freightliner had, before being loaded onto a train, to be fitted with stanchions at about two feet intervals down the sides and along the back of the loading area. Between the stanchions were fitted pieces of ply wood, usually six ply. The reason for these stanchions and boards was to limit the effect of winds on the sheeting especially when the train entered a railway tunnel and the speed of the train caused a partial vacuum into which may be sucked any loose edges of sheeting. Before delivery of a load to a customer, these boards and stanchions had to be removed and stored in a special store for ropes, sheets, stanchions and boards within the terminal.

All the Freightliner terminals in the country had one of these drive through bays where ropes, sheets stanchions and boards were stored in a wooden hut. The drive through was at trailer floor height and was approximately six inches wider than a heavy goods vehicle. It had a platform on either side, which was approximately six feet wide, to work from. The man in charge of the bay at Trafford Park terminal was a black guy by the name of Byron, whose son, after passing his HGV; test, also drove for Freightliners as did Dick Wilson's son and one or two others. I sometimes think that the railway's motto should have been 'Nepotism Rules, OK.'

On the day in question, which was a snowy, icy and unusually cold January day, I was stripping the stanchions and boards from my load. While I was thus employed Dick Wilson left the terminal prior to me and so arrived at the Stubbins' Paper Mills before me. When I arrived at the mills holding area, Dick had already been pulled round to the unloading bay and so I started to undo the the ropes, which held my load, in readiness for unloading.

The ropes were frozen stiff and I was experiencing difficulty gripping them with rubber gloves on. I removed my gloves and started to physically undo each dolly around the load. The dolly is a quick release knot used to tighten ropes on a load but because of the frozen state of the ropes the dollies would not release. By the time I had manually undone them all my fingertips were raw and bleeding. I put my gloves back on, for a little protection, and started to pull the ropes off the load. Lo and behold the ropes were frozen to the sheets.

I clambered onto the top of the load via the catwalk and headboard. The surface of the sheets was like a snow covered ice skating rink and so, with a great deal of care, I got down on all fours and worked my way along the top of the load pulling the ropes through the ice until they were all free. Then, with my overalls and trousers soaked through, I half climbed, and half stumbled down the headboard onto the cat walk and back down to ground level. Still with some difficulty, I pulled all the ropes off the load. It was impossible to fold them up, just then, because of their frozen state, so I left them where they lay for the time being.

More of the same was encountered when I came to undo the sheet ties. They too were tied down and secured with dollies, which is not quite *de rigueur* when roping and sheeting. Even with my industrial gloves on my hands had become numb and so it took quite a while to undo all the sheet ties. Finally I had them all undone and off the hooks. I then unravelled the sheets and undid the dog ears and front and rear envelopes in readiness for pulling them from the load.

In despair and close to tears and cursing rather volubly I was surprised to see Dick as he appeared around the corner and believe me I was never so glad to see another driver. My cursing and swearing was something that Dick found rather humorous and hearing me shouting at the ropes and sheets that they were the *'fornicating, illegitimate, male offspring of copulating dogs,'* he came over to me and with a grin on his face he said, 'Don't you know that talking and cursing to yourself is one of the first signs of madness?' Now let's get these sheets off.'

With that he took hold of one of the corners of the rear sheet and I gripped the other. Together we tugged and pulled and finally the frozen tarpaulin gave up its hold on the load and came free. Showers of sheet ice and snow rained down upon us as it came off the back of the load. We pulled until the whole sheet came off at the rear of the trailer and hit the ground in the same shape as if it was still covering the load. It was only the weight of the remaining ice, snow and water that caused it to collapse in a misshapen heap on the floor.

It was then time to remove the front sheet. This we did by pulling it from the side of the vehicle, once again ice and snow showered down upon us. The front sheet came off the load a little easier and a little flatter than the rear one. Once it was off we turned it over to remove any excess ice. We then turned it back again and with great difficulty, managed to fold it. It was then time to attack the remaining sheet and after about twenty minutes we had both sheets folded and stowed on the rear end of the trailer. The ropes had to be stamped and trodden on to soften them up and finally when they had lost most of their frozen rigidity we them wrapped up. Both of us had to remove our topcoats, which were soaked through. I immediately hung mine in my cab with the heater blowing hot air at full blast and Dick, upon returning to his vehicle, did the same with his. I thanked Dick profusely for the help he had rendered and he then went to see how the unloading of his trailer was progressing. I went to the gents toilets to wash the blood from my hands which were now throbbing after the numbness had subsided. I ran my hands under warm water in an effort to alleviate the painful throbbing. The pain was excruciating and I cannot remember having experienced agony and pulsating like it.

Once Dick was unloaded and I had recovered some normal feeling to my hands I reversed my trailer onto the loading bay and the foreman in charge of despatch and receiving then took me to the mill's medical centre where my bloodied fingers were cleansed and dressed as best as was possible.

After all this messing about with frozen sheets and ropes, clambering on and off the slippery load and feeling as if my body had been invaded by Arctic permafrost, it took no more than fifteen minutes to unload my trailer.

So do not let anyone try to tell you that driving heavy goods vehicles for a living is an easy option. Driving is only part of the job.

Upon my return to the terminal I had started to sniffle and my nose was running; a slight cough had developed which manifested itself as a tickle at the back of my throat that caused me to retch, splutter and convulse. As the day went on the cough became a hacking, cutting cough and got much worse and by the end of the working day I was coughing and expectorating relentlessly.

By the time I had gotten home from work and as the evening drew on, the hacking had become harsher. With each cough it felt as if someone had poured a strong acid down my throat and was trying to scorch my lungs from their position within my chest cavity. Each cough brought a searing pain as though the strong acid had been heated to a white hot temperature and was trying to burn its way through my chest. By then I was expelling more and more unhealthy globules of brightly coloured sputum which made me feel quite nauseous.

My wife served me my evening meal but, appetising and tasty as it looked, I was unable to eat much more than a couple of forksful and as the evening progressed to night I began to feel worse. My symptoms now included a blinding headache; I realised that the best thing I could do was to take a couple of aspirins with a hot drink, put on my pyjamas and retire to bed. Sleep came in snatches interspersed with bouts of rasping, retching and coughing and come the dawn, as the alarm clock started to play its shrill, cacophonous reveille, I was already awake having slept fitfully and having probably accumulated no more than two hours of slumber.

Feeling somewhat debilitated and still weary due to the lack of proper sleep I threw the blankets back and put my legs over the side of the bed. With difficulty, I pulled myself up into a sitting position and was overcome by light-headedness and I became aware of a heavy limbed feeling. My arms and legs seemed reluctant to obey orders from my brain. I stood up and my feet felt as if they were enclosed in a pair of divers, lead-weighted boots.

After struggling and failing to don some clothing I stumbled, in my pyjamas, heavy footed, like a slow moving, drunken man, downstairs where firstly, I put the kettle on. I then phoned Freightliner to inform them that I would not be attending work that day. I cannot remember who answered the phone that morning but after the usual 'good Mornings', I said 'I am very sorry, but I will not be in today due to fact that I have developed a heavy cold and a terrible cough. I believe that my symptoms are due to the conditions under which I was expected to work yesterday at Stubbins' Paper Mill.'

'O.K.' was the reply, 'We'll cover your job. Keep us informed as to your progress, Good bye.'

When the short conversation had finished I returned to the kitchen and poured the boiled water into a mug and made a cup of tea. Returning to the sitting room with my infusion I lit the gas fire and sat down to drink my scalding brew. As I sat down I realised that I was sweating excessively and at the same time shivering quite violently. My whole body was racked by violent tremors and an efflux of perspiration dripped from my brow. My once runny nose was now as dry as the proverbial bone but was not allowing any inspiration of air and I was forced to breathe through my mouth.

Just as I had finished my cup of tea my wife came down the stairs. She came over and stood before me, with a look of incredulity upon her face she uttered the words 'Bloody Hell! You look bloody awful.'

I acknowledged and concurred with her comment with a slight nod of my head, which was about all I could manage.

'Come on,' said my beloved, 'lets get you back to bed.'

She reached out to help me stand. But# even as I gave it my best effort, as I rose from the seat my legs buckled beneath me and I fell, untidily to the floor.

'I'm going to phone the doctor,' said my wife 'but first I'll make a bed up for you on the settee.

After my couchette had been made and I had struggled to clamber between the sheets, the doctor was called. Lying in the made up bed, cocooned in its warmth, I was shivering, sweating and retching. Each cough tore me apart and I lay there feeling terribly sorry for myself.

The doctor arrived just before noon. He thoroughly examined me and diagnosed influenza of which ever strain was doing the rounds at the time. My temperature was taken and found to be one hundred and two degrees Fahrenheit instead of the usual ninety eight point six. He recommended plenty of fluids and bed rest and prescribed a proprietary brand of expectorant to help to alleviate the retching and coughing, plus two paracetamol tablets every four hours. He then made out a sick note for a two week period and that was as much as he could do for me.

That was the only time that I have suffered from full blown flu but it made me think that those people who continue to smoke and go to work saying that they have the flu most certainly do not have the flu. They may have a heavy or bad cold but they do not have the flu. Influenza is a killer, a decimator of populations, a very serious and debilitating disease, especially as it affects the old and the infirm. After the first Great War (1914–18) there was a flu pandemic that killed more people than four and a half years of trench warfare killed, so do not ever treat flu lightly.

Over seven days the symptoms receded and as I slowly recovered I was able to return to the marital bed, but it was to be another week before I was fit enough to contemplate a return to work. Influenza strikes quickly and recedes slowly. At the onset of the disease I was reduced to a quivering, shivering wreck, as weak as a new born child. At one point I could barely lift my arms, perambulation was impossible and I lost eleven pounds in weight. Influenza is better than any diet for the overweight.

When I at last returned to work I was still in a weakened state and overall it probably took another three weeks to regain the weight that I had lost and to return to the level of fitness that I had enjoyed before I fell ill.

DODGY NIGHTS OUT

I was once sent to a storage depot that belonged to McVitie Biscuits, to pick up a load and return with it to the Freightliner depot. When I arrived at the storage facility, which was at Measham just off the A42 in Leicestershire and served as a storage depot for McVitie's Ashby-de- la-Douche bakery/factory, I found a queue of vehicles waiting to be loaded.

I finally got loaded at about 1730hrs and received my notes at 1800hrs. It was now too late to legally return to the Freightliner terminal and so I had to book a night out. I phoned the transport office to let them know what was happening but actually booked off in my log book at the Salt Box Café on the old A50, where I called in for an overnight parking ticket and then ran home on a dodgy.

I parked the Seddon that I was driving on that day on some spare land nearby to where I lived. The land was just around the corner from my abode and was clear of houses due to the demolition of numerous terraced houses, The result of a Compulsory Purchase Order. The rear doors of the container were sealed with a heavy duty custom's seal so I locked my unit and went home.

The next morning I returned to my vehicle to find that the passenger door had been forced open, the lock and door handle were broken and a few personal items had been taken, though luckily nothing of any value was missing. I walked around the vehicle to do a visual check and noticed that the custom seal had been tampered with but not broken.

There were a couple of hanks of rope hung at the rear of my cab and I had to use one of these to secure the door. I tied one end to the internal door handle and wrapped the rope around the driving seat and pulled the door closed via a dolly which I tied off around the base of the gear stick. I then drove the vehicle to the street where I lived and parked up outside my home. Next, I telephoned the depot and pretended that I was still at the Salt Box Café and that my vehicle had been broken into there. The transport manager asked if the vehicle was drivable to which I responded in the affirmative. My instructions were to then return to the depot *tout suite* to despatch the container and have the damage to the vehicle assessed. Extensive remedial work to the door pillar and a new door was prescribed. I handed in my overnight parking ticket for reimbursement and picked up my overnight subsistence money and was allocated another vehicle.

[4]Another instance of a stupid dodgy night out occurred when I was sent, with a forty feet container to Billingham near Middlesbrough and I could not be loaded until the following day. Because I had no money or night out gear with me I foolishly went home with another driver, in his truck and thumbed my way back the next day. Yet another dodgy occurred when I was given a container that had missed its train, late in the afternoon,

---

4. A fuller and more descriptive account of these incidents can be found in the earlier book 'This Truckin' Life'

to deliver to Holyhead Freightliner terminal. I pocketed the night out money and ran the vehicle home and set off at about 0300hrs the next morning. That incident involved the Ministry, the police and a vehicle check.

Nights spent away from the depot were infrequent at Freightliner and thus dodgy nights out were even less infrequent. Most of the trips were within a fifty mile radius from the terminal. There was only myself and one or two others who would willingly do nights out and these only occurred when a container arrived late for its train. If that box was deemed important and for a time sensitive delivery it would be sent to its destination by road.

THE NUR AND THE RMT

When I first joined the railway at Deansgate I was, on my second day, approached by the union rep. The union was the NUR (National Union of Railwaymen), and had been for years. The footplate men i.e. train drivers and firemen belonged to the ASLEF union and railway's clerical staff had their own union. Unions in those days operated on a closed shop basis, if you weren't in the union you didn't work or you were treated as scab labour. I joined the union.

The NUR operated at all the railway depots nationally and all employees were union members. This extended to all the allied companies that belonged to the railways, although some companies had dual union representation such as BRS and Pickford's where one could join either the TGWU or the NUR Other companies that came under the railway's umbrella like NCL Freightliner and later Lynx and EXEL were solely NUR camps and latterly RMT (The National Union of Rail, Maritime and Transport Workers).

The RMT is the NUR renamed and was the largest union within the transport sector, until the amalgamation of TGWU and Amicus in 2007, and has members in the whole

of the rail network including the London underground. The majority of the road transport that is allied to the rail system and has contracts with most of the big national companies has the RMT as its main union. Certain shipping allows its workers membership of the RMT Even in these days when unions have lost a lot of their power since a certain Lady Thatcher, with her far, right wing views, tried to virtually destroy unions within the workforce and whereby union membership is not compulsory, most workers can see the benefits of membership of a large union. Protection from unscrupulous bosses, legal representation, cheap, private health care and discounts on a multiplicity of commodities are available through union membership.

Whenever I left the railway and returned at a later date I would renew my union membership.

The man in charge of union business at Freightliner was the late Harry Kelshaw. Harry was a dedicated union man with the plight of the working man deep within his heart. He was ably assisted by three drivers, Jimmy Toole, Ernie Price and Eric Cartledge, all good union men, although I believe there was once a case of some misappropriation of union funds or maybe it was something more innocent like vote rigging, whatever it was there was an investigation. After the investigation all parties were cleared, but as is the norm in these types of case, a cloud hung over certain officers and a lot of trust was lost. When thrown, mud has a tendency to stick. Because of his integrity, the finger of suspicion never lighted on Harry Kelshaw.

CHAPTER 15
BACK TO THE RAILWAY
AS A GUARD

I left Freightliner and the railways to take up a job with Brain Haulage from Grays in Essex. This in hindsight was a foolish move. The remuneration at Brain's was half again what I was earning at Freightliner and the subsistence money was a couple of quid more for each night spent away from home but the job was only short lived and lasted only two years. After another year or so taking work as I could get it I ended up working for nine years for British Telecom.

I was medically retired from British Telecom plc; after an industrial accident. This accident resulted in me suffering a pelvic fracture and some lower spinal, soft tissue damage from which I still suffer.

I was unable to work for a while and when I finally felt fit enough to return to driving I worked part time for different agencies, a couple of days a week because, at the time, that was all I could manage. One of the agencies I did some work for was BRS Taskforce.

I was sat at home one evening perusing the situations vacant in the Manchester Evening News when my eyes fell upon an advertisement for vacancies for the position of conductor/guard on First North West trains working out of Manchester, Piccadilly Station. I applied for the post and received a reply that offered me an interview. I attended the interview, sat an assessment examination and was selected to serve as a trainee conductor/ guard.

The training course was a twelve weeks, class room based course with occasional days out in the field learning about buckeye couplings and the operation of trains.

On one occasion the whole class, with our teacher, went down to Llandudno by train as an on the job learning day. We also visited marshalling yards at Liverpool and Crewe. We had a number of other days visiting different railway premises in different towns.

There were three women amongst a class of fifteen, one of them a skinny, slip of a girl, the rest were of the male gender although one of the men was a little feminine in his ways to say the least. Within the role of conductor/guard there are some quite physical aspects to be dealt with. One such is the coupling and uncoupling of rolling stock where the air lines have to be connected along with the electrical connection. The buck eye coupling has to be lifted and locked into place. These things are done in reverse when uncoupling.

The buck eye coupling has been in use for numerous years because it has proved itself to be secure and safe. It is, however, a heavy piece of equipment and it was on the day that we were being trained in its use that the rather effeminate chap amongst our ranks failed dismally.

We were sent to a marshalling yard somewhere in the Merseyside area with our teacher, who himself was a Scouser, to be instructed on how to safely connect two items of rolling stock which were equipped with the buck eye coupling. At first we gathered around a static railway carriage and our teacher went about demonstrating how to lift the buck eye and lock it in position and how to release it and lower it to its position when not in use.

The teacher then called us forward one at a time to attempt that which had just been demonstrated. Three of the males, eager to show off their strength, ran forward to attempt the task and each succeeded.

From the distaff side the next person to be called forward was the slim slip of a girl. She stepped toward the coupling, gripped it as shown and with a lot of effort completed what was required of her.

It was then the effeminate guys turn to have a go. He minced towards the coupling tossing his hair back and whispering something about broken nails. He stopped and looked at the coupling and then tentatively reached for it. His first task was to lift it and lock it into position. He pulled at it, wrestled with it, cursed it, bur barely moved it an inch. He turned around and looked pleadingly at the teacher who said 'Come on you fuckin' big Nancy boy, You ain't gonna let a li'l girl like this beat you are you?' he asked pointing at the girl. 'Give it another go.'

'Do I have to do it?' he asked. 'I just wanted to take fares and please people and work the trains between stations. Nobody told me that I'd have to do all this dirty work.'

'Well you either do it or fuck off back to Manchester and look for another job, cos you're no good to me if you can't couple up.'

'Oooh', replied the Nancy boy, 'I can couple up OK but not the way that you mean.'

He attempted to lift the coupling a second time but fell to his knees. The rest of the guys were laughing at the weakling but the girls went to his assistance because, I suppose, they were kindred spirits. The rest of us completed the task and continued the day's training. The next task was the actual coupling and uncoupling of the air lines and electrical connections between two railway carriages that were already in tandem. We then all returned to

Manchester where the young failure was told that he was not fit for the course and sent on his way.

The classroom was where we had to learn all the theory. We learnt about single line workings, engineering works, track closures, including knowledge of PICOW's and PICOP's. These were Person in Charge of Works and Person in Charge of Possession. We were also instructed in the safety of the train and its passengers, the laying of warning detonators in case of an emergency and a multiplicity of other necessary things. We also had to learn about trackside speed restrictions and warning boards such as the whistle board and on track warning devices such as the Automatic Warning Device (AWD). A good knowledge of signalling, both semaphore and electrical was instilled into the brains of the trainees. The operation of the different types of trains that we were to work on had to be learnt including those with automatic doors and also those of slam door stock which were still in operation. The conductor/guards rule book had to be read, revised and absorbed thoroughly. The conductors computerised ticket machine also had to be mastered.

At the end of all this force fed knowledge was an examination whereby seventy per cent had to be gained for a pass. Luckily on the course that I attended everyone passed. When we first went out on the trains it was with an experienced conductor and road learning was the order of the day. Road learning was gaining of knowledge of the route one was to be on and one had to road learn every new route that one was to operate. This meant knowing every station on the road in the order along the route, thus allowing time to get back to the guards van in order to give the driver the signal to move off. The reason it was called road learning stems from the time when the railways were known as railroads.

In essence it is the conductor/guard who has responsibility for the train. It is he who dictates when the train can move off and the driver will not move until he has the requisite signal from the guard. If there is an emergency such as a fire or a derailment or a mechanical breakdown it is the conductor who has to lead the passengers to a place of safety and lay warning devices for any oncoming trains.

In my short time as guard, fortunately, I was never called upon to lead passengers to a place of safety because of a breakdown, derailment or any other incident but there were other types of incident that happened whilst collecting fares.

One morning, on a relatively empty train, on the Liverpool, Lime Street road, I came across a surly, unkempt youth. The scruffy, long haired adolescent was slouched in a half lying position with his feet on the opposite seat and he was smoking a cigarette in a non smoking carriage. I approached the lad, who was casually cleaning his finger nails with the pointed blade of a switchblade knife. My intention, as I drew close to this young, knife wielding passenger, was to ask for his ticket and request that he remove his feet from the seating and to put out his cigarette.

When I was stood by his side, he nonchalantly flashed his ticket at me. The ticket was checked by me and found to be a legitimate permit to travel as far as Liverpool so I said, 'Thank you now would you mind removing your feet from the seating and would you please put out your cigarette as this is a non smoking carriage?'

'Would you mind fuckin' off?' he replied, twirling the knife between his fingers, 'an' leave me alone.'

Just at that time a tall, well built, middle aged gentleman approached. He was dressed like a business man in a neat, dark suit. He stood at my side and said to the obnoxious youth, 'Why don't you do as the guard as asked?'

The response was 'Why don't you do as I ask and join the guard and fuck off? Who the fuck are you anyway? You nosey bastard.'

With this the gentleman's hand went to the inside pocket of his jacket and brought out a wallet which he flipped open to show the young yob, I am Sergeant ....? of the British Transport Police.' He said, 'and that knife that you are brandishing is an illegal and offensive weapon. You are under arrest and I am holding you until we arrive at Liverpool, Lime Street where you will be handed over to the city's police force for questioning. If you try to abscond or resist arrest, be sure that I will physically restrain you. Now hand over that weapon'

The juvenile delinquent, once so insolent and sure of his self had then lost all of his cockiness and brashness. He became a quivering, apologetic child. His feet were once more on the floor and his cigarette had been extinguished. He begged the officer as he handed him the knife. 'Please sir, let me off this once and I'll never cause any bother again, please. Mi mam said she'd kill me if I got in trouble again.'

But the Transport Bobby would have none of it. 'You have sworn at both me and this conductor who is going about the job he is paid to do. Brandishing a flick knife can be taken as threatening behaviour. His job is hard enough without the likes of you or undesirable characters of your sort making it more difficult. So I am taking it unto myself to make an example of you and hope that you might learn a lesson from it.' With that he sat down next to the youth and phoned the Liverpool constabulary. Upon arriving at Liverpool, Lime Street he escorted the sullen, mumbling, trouble causer into the arms of the waiting police for them to deal with.

Isn't it amusing how the immature, ruffians of this world when confronted by a figure of authority, seem to lose their self confidence and aggressive nature. I, dressed in my conductor's uniform, had posed no threat to the young hoodlum armed with a blade. He did not see me as the face of authority, but the sight of an official warrant card, displayed by a police officer, albeit a British Transport Police Officer caused him to quake in his trainers.

The selling of tickets or permits to travel is another of the conductor's responsibilities and to give incentive to this task a commission was paid on ticket sales. Passengers were and are supposed to by their tickets before boarding but in the rush hour that is not always possible, hence the ticket sales on board.

Not long after I had started as a guard and I was working a train without any guidance from another guard I discovered that some people have a strange and perverse sense of humour. I was working the Glossop line out of Piccadilly when two chaps boarded at Godley, an unmanned station. Until the two men boarded, the train had been empty of passengers. Once I had given the signal for the train to move off I approached the two passengers with the greeting 'Good morning guys, could I have your fares please?'

'We're not paying. The bloody fares are too high.' Was the response that I received for my polite enquiry. The larger of the two who resembled a pugilistic gladiator with shoulders like a silverback gorilla and a brow like Frankenstein's monster with a broken nose and cauliflower ear said 'So what the fuck are you gonna do about it. Go on what you gonna fuckin' do about it?!'

'Come on fellers,' I said 'I'm only trying to earn a living.'

And with that I walked away rather than risk an altercation that I thought might have dire consequences for my person. When I was approximately half way to the driver's compartment the two men started laughing loudly and said, 'Here you are mate. Hang on a minute, we're only joking. We knew, because we hadn't seen you before, that you're probably new on the job and we thought we'd have a bit of a laugh. No offence, pal, all right?'

They then paid their fares in full and told me to keep the change in consolation for their joke. The change wasn't much and I would sooner they had paid their fares without the so called humour but what the heck, it was all in a day's work for the average guard cum conductor.

There have been times I have known conductors not to bother selling tickets, especially on the late night, week-end trains where loutish behaviour by the younger, drunken adults of this country, can dictate that the conductor locks him or herself in the guards van rather than suffer the wrath of gangs of drunken hooligans. Guards have been assaulted in the past and the trains fixtures and fittings have been thrown through the windows of trains. Those occurrences were usually on trains returning to Piccadilly station and noticeably on the last train from Chester. When the train pulled into Piccadilly station the ruffians and hooligans were quite surprised to find the Transport Police waiting for them. Those vandals and villains thought that there was no communication between train and station. Those poor ill informed idiots had a rude awakening on arrival at Piccadilly.

Conductors that were diligent and keen would do their best to ensure that everyone had a ticket; others would sell just enough to justify their jobs. Sometimes a customer on a local train would ask for a ticket to London or Glasgow or any other far flung destination. Those ticket sales were like manna from heaven to the conductor who had to work out the best route and cheapest fare for the journey. The commission for one ticket sale to the metropolis was as much as one could hope to earn selling numerous local tickets all day.

Some passengers would go to extraordinary lengths to avoid buying a ticket. It was not unusual for some commuters to board a train and make straight for the toilet where they would lock themselves in. Not coming out until the train pulled into their required station when they would make a hurried exit. Others would continually change carriages in an attempt to avoid the guard at all costs.

If I was having a conscientious day I would wait outside the toilet and hopefully catch the fare dodger. These people when caught red handed usually paid up although the odd one would occasionally barge past and flee down the platform. If I saw the type of traveller that changed carriages to avoid paying I would follow him or her doggedly and they would usually realise the game was up and pay. It was like a game to those fare dodgers and it became a case of some you won, some you lost.

RAILWAY SHIFTS

Although I had worked shift work in the past nothing prepared me for the shift system employed by the train services. Start times were dictated by the movement of rolling stock so that if ones first train was to leave the station at 0332hrs the starting time for the guard would be half an hour before i.e. 0302hrs: to enable him or her to get their traps and book out a ticket machine and hopefully time to have a quick cup of tea. Granted, one would be finished for 1100hrs but those starting times were neither days nor nights and there could be a different starting time every day of the week. It took a lot of getting used to, going to bed while it was still light because one had to rise at 0200hrs.

The late shifts were as bad with starting times from noon up to 2100 hrs where after it was deemed a night shift. A conductor's shift, or indeed any other person working for the rail services, including drivers and other personnel such as platform and station staff, could fall on a Bank Holiday and he or she would be paid extra for that shift but it was still considered their normal shift as I found out when my late shift fell on New Year's Eve and I didn't finish until 0100hrs on New Years day.

TERMINATION

I actually got sacked from my job as a conductor. The reason for this was fare evasion. I was working out of the Manchester Airport station at the time and I normally went to work in my car. For some reason on the day in question I travelled to Piccadilly and caught the Airport train. Staff that had been employed by the railways for years continued to get free travel on the trains, but they were phased out for new starters. Being a new starter meant that I did not get these concessions.

That seemed a totally unfair system to me, to have people working alongside one another, doing the same job and one of them has benefits and concessions that could be worth thousands of pounds per annum and the other gets no concessions at all. Of course, like any private industry where profit comes before the welfare of the staff, it was just a long term, cost cutting exercise. As and when the older staff, that are in receipt of these concessions, leave or retire the concessions will be totally phased out amongst the manual grades, although you can bet your life on it that the top managerial staff will keep theirs.

The guard on the train I caught on this day was one of the guys that had done his training with me. I offered him the fare and he said, 'You're all right, put your money away.'

I said 'Thanks a lot; I'll do the same for you one day.'

What I didn't know was we were being watched by a guy called Adrian who had also trained with us but had then transferred to the Revenue Protection Squad, a sort of in house police force meant to catch fare dodgers.

As I got off the train at the Airport station Adrian approached me and asked 'Do you mind if I look at your ticket, please?' knowing full well that I didn't have one.

I replied, 'Bloody hell, Adrian, we're supposed to be mates. I'm not the enemy, you know. You're supposed to be out there catching persistent fare dodgers, not your work mates.'

'I'm sorry,' he replied 'I'm just doing my job. I'd like you to accompany me back to Piccadilly where we can sort this out. I'll just go and tell your supervisor what's happening.'

I had no option but to return to Piccadilly Station with Adrian. On the return journey he attempted to make conversation with me, but I mostly ignored him except for the once when I said, 'Fuck off.' In response to his question. I could not, however, help but listen to his one sided conversation as he asked: 'Don't you think that it's ironic that I travel the rails all day without paying, whilst trying to catch people travelling the rails all day without paying?' When we arrived at Piccadilly I was escorted to the manager's office to be greeted by my line manager, who after a brief interview with both me and Adrian immediately suspended me and told me to hand in my traps. I then went home and waited for the outcome.

One week later I received a phone call to attend a disciplinary hearing at Piccadilly where the case against me was read out in front of a panel of managers. One of whom commented that 'Fare evasion is a major concern for First North West Railways and your case has been thoroughly discussed and reviewed.' and then asked 'Have you anything to say in your defence?'

Well, what could I say? I had not paid the requisite fare and I had been caught. I did not want to implicate the conductor who had refused my offer to pay and so I said

'I have nothing to say except that I believe that I have truly learnt my lesson and that it won't happen again.'

'Too bloody right it won't happen again.' said my boss, 'because you won't be working here any longer. The panel has decided that because of your dishonesty you do not have the necessary requirements and integrity to work for First North West trains and so your contract will be terminated forthwith. Think yourself lucky that this has not become a case for the police and the courts. All that is left for you to do is return all of your uniform as soon as possible. Now you may vacate the premises. Adrian will escort you off the station.'

The conductor who had refused my offer to pay was also reported by Adrian but he was given a severe reprimand and kept his job. My attempt not to implicate him made no difference at all when dealing with a jobsworth like Adrian. So that was that, I was out of work again and a branded fare dodger. Oh what a stigma to bear.

CHAPTER 16
RETURN TO DRIVING

BRS TASKFORCE

Unemployment did not reign long, The feeling that things might not quite work out at First North West Railway was uppermost in my mind and so pre-empting the actions of First North West's management I arranged an interview, with BRS Taskforce. BRS was another company that had been allied to the Railway's since the nationalisation of inland transport after the Second World War. The interview took place during the week that I was on suspension from the First North West Railway Company and was conducted, rather fortuitously, by a chap named Wayne, with whom I had worked prior. A position as driver, Class One, was offered and I commenced my employment with BRS on the following Monday, seven days from the day that I was sacked from First North West Railway.

BRS Taskforce, being one of the companies that came into the fold of railway companies, supplied drivers for all the companies and contracts that were once serviced by the railways and BRS haulage, the only difference being that the majority of the freight, nowadays, went by road.

My first assignment for BRS was as a class one driver for EXEL Logistics, once NCL, on their automotive contract. My starting time was 0700 and when I pulled into the yard in Trafford Park on the Monday morning I was surprised to see numerous drivers that I had known on the railway. These drivers were still members of the RMT and some of them had worked for the railway for forty years or more and like me had passed their original driving tests at the BR School of Driving on the Scammell Scarab. Because they had been with the company through thick and thin, through good times and bad and through a number of name changes and even a management buy out, these men still held their railway concessions of free travel and free continental travel. Albeit they would all be retired within the next ten years and their concessions phased out.

That first morning I was allocated a brand new truck leased through BRS Truck Rental and put on the Rover/BMW/Mini contract which constituted taking a pre loaded trailer down to the Rover factory at Longbridge, Birmingham, tipping and reloading and returning to the Trafford Park depot where the load would be transhipped onto various trailers and four wheelers for various destinations on the night trunk or for the next day. The overall round trip on the run that I was on was approximately six hours although I was guaranteed eight hours.

Another job assigned to me on the automotive contract was the Rover/BMW factory at Cowley, Oxford. I only did this job when there was no one else to do it and this was not by choice. The reason that I did not like the Cowley run was that because of the traffic and the distance involved plus the waiting in queues to tip and reload the job almost always entailed a fourteen or fifteen hour day and occasionally an overnight stay. To be honest, after a lifetime in haulage and being away from home a great deal of the time, day work was now my preference and preferably no more than nine or ten hours a day. I did not want nor need the overtime and generally EXEL would try to accommodate me.

If I knew beforehand and was prepared I would do nights out. The company would, of course, have to give me twenty four hours notice.

Other contracts that were once served by the railways and BRS haulage were Dunlop Tyres, Pirelli Tyres, Prince's Foods, Newsflow, Crazy George's Furniture now Brighthouse, The Hotpoint company, Hoover, Daewoo, Kellogg's, various brewers, North West Water now United Utilities and more , all of which I have worked on at one time or another.

It was whilst working on the North West Water contract that a full time post arose and the job was offered to me. I accepted in the knowledge that working for a company full time is better and more secure than working for an agency even if that agency supplied drivers to all the railway related companies.

THE NORTH WEST WATER CONTRACT

Two years was the length of time I spent working on the NWW contract for EXEL Logistics. During this time it became known as the United Utility contract when the North West Water Board and the North West Electricity Board amalgamated. It was the only depot and contract, that I knew of, belonging to EXEL that had no union representation and so I set the wheels in motion to rectify that situation. I canvassed all the staff on their views on union membership. They in turn asked me how union membership would benefit them. I explained, as best as I was able, the numerous benefits available to union members. Over and above the free legal advice from the union's appointed solicitor's, security of tenure within the workplace and monetary gains which may be obtained there were other benefits that included discounts on various commodities, training courses, cheaper car and house insurance and flights amongst a multiplicity of others.

The first major step that could be put right was the upgrading of the overtime rates at the depot. EXEL, NWW was the only depot that still paid the old railway rate of time and one quarter for overtime. All other depots paid time and one half. I approached the management about this anomaly and got nowhere. It was then that I broached the subject of union membership with the depot management. Surprisingly, management agreed that if there was sufficient interest then they could not and would not attempt to stop the workforce joining a union.

My next step was to approach the local office of the preferred union, which happened to be the TGWU my personal choice was the RMT but I had to do as the majority demanded. This I did and within a month all manual employees at the depot were *bona fide* union members, having their contributions paid through their wages. I became the shop steward and put into motion negotiations for the upgrading of the overtime rate with a limited amount of back pay. We won this first round of negotiations and it seemed that I could do no wrong. The workers were more willing to work overtime hours for an enhanced rate of pay.

There were two class one driver's at the depot , myself and an ex North west Electricity Board worker called Mel who had accepted redundancy from NWEB and ended up doing the same job with EXEL for a lower wage but with a lump sum of money in the bank. There were also a number of four wheeler curtainsiders for smaller deliveries. There were no nights out on this job. The furthest we went in a northerly direction was Carlisle and the Cumbrian coast and we rarely went further than Stoke on the south side. We covered Merseyside and the Wirral, with occasional forays into Yorkshire and Northumbria. The trips that were outside the North West Water area were usually to other water and electricity companies.

My job within the company was the delivery of all North West Water and North West Electricity Board stores to all the depots within the region. These deliveries were by way of replenishment of stores that had been used. We also delivered to contractors' depots and to sites where contractors were working. Also involved was the collection of returns and faulty equipment not to mention the collection of empty pallets which could be sold on to give a small separate income.

Things were going swimmingly when I suffered a series of unexplained black outs. I went to my doctor who reported these losses of consciousness to the DVLA who, in their wisdom and probably quite rightly so, revoked my vocational license. Luckily they left me with my ordinary driver's license which still allowed me to drive the fifteen miles to work.

EXEL, being an ex-railway company, generally, is a company that looks after its workforce and considering the problems I was undergoing, they treated me as well as could be expected. Rather than finish me there and then on health grounds the depot manager appointed me as the Health and Safety Officer for the depot. I was sent to Birmingham, for a week, on a residential Health and Safety course and then became responsible for risk assessments and up dating the workforce, both clerical and manual, upon the advancements in health and safety in the workplace and all other health and safety issues.

My responsibilities included giving talks on manual handling and running courses on that subject in an attempt to lower the incidence of industrial accidents caused by using the wrong method of lifting etc. I was also responsible for COSSH (the Control of Substances Hazardous to Health) which included a multiplicity of substances from cleaning materials and thinners to every day use of diesel and butane gas. I had to re-establish dedicated walk ways in the warehouse and was in charge of tidiness and cleanliness in the depot.

The office staff also came to me with their grievances about the length of time sat in front of a computer screen and about access to free eyesight tests. Other complaints ranged from the type of seating and the use of footrests whilst sat at their work stations. What was the course of action to take if repetitive strain injury was suspected was a regular enquiry plus a multitude of other work related topics? Of course there were no guarantees or a universal panacea for any of these complaints, everything, to a certain degree, was at the whim of the management.

A fork lift truck refresher course was the next step to enable me to load and unload the delivery vehicles and contractor's vehicles. Most of the warehouse staff had fork lift truck licenses and so I very rarely had to use the stacker trucks. After finishing the FLT course it was considered sensible to send me on a first aid course and allow me to become one of the depots first aiders.

All the courses that I was sent on were within the company's time and at the company's expense. Each course was at least a week long and whilst I was on each course I was, of course, non productive. EXEL paid me my full wages plus meal allowance while I was in the course of bettering myself, albeit for the company's benefit and after the laying out of so much expense I later became a little disillusioned that there was no future for me within the company.

Amongst my other responsibilities, while I was confined to yard duties, was the banding of awkward loads onto pallets to ensure their safety in transit. The shunting of vehicles about the yard, If necessary, was allocated to me. It was only when I had a black out within the workplace that my situation was reviewed. Fork lift and shunting duties immediately became no go situations and I was told not to work within close proximity of moving vehicles. Basically all I could do was my health and safety duties and these did not fill a working day.

A report on my physical health and its shortcomings had been forwarded to the company's higher management for further discussion. The depot manager requested my presence and then related to me the decision of the higher management within the company. That decision was that I was not fulfilling the duties that I was employed to do, i.e. driving duties and that there was not enough work of another kind to keep me fully employed. He carried on by saying 'It is with great regret that I have to let you go. You have been an asset to the company. If it was in any way possible to find you work within the depot on a class one driver's rate, then I would. Unfortunately, I can't and the only thing I can do which I can see benefiting you monetarily is to suggest medical retirement from EXEL. This will entitle you to your pension rights and a lump sum which I hope will help soften the blow of this decision.'

The manager and I talked a little longer and he suggested that he make an appointment with the company doctor to legitimise the decision to terminate my employment on medical grounds. We both agreed that his suggestion was the best way forward. I was to leave the depot immediately and wait for an appointment to see the occupational health board. I said goodbye to the others in the depot and then drove home.

Everything seemed to be pushed through rather quickly and before long I had been to see the EXEL company doctor and certified unfit to carry out my job and my employment on the NWW contract came to an end and indeed my employment with EXEL and all other Railway's related companies terminated on that day. I would be paid wages in lieu of notice plus what holiday pay I had accrued plus a lump sum and then a small pension for life. So there I was, out of work with no LGV license and no immediate hope of getting it reinstated.

BACK TO BRS TASKFORCE

After undergoing numerous medical examinations and wearing a heart monitor for a year the hospital staff and other medical luminaries could not find anything wrong with me. It was concluded that I had suffered a number of unexplained faints to which there seemed to be no contributing factors. My blood pressure was OK, my heartbeat showed no arrhythmia, my heart in general was OK, and there were no irregularities in my brain activity. It seemed that all my internal plumbing was alright and my electrical circuits were wired up just fine. All medical documentation was sent to the DVLA and I was given the all clear to re-apply for my LGV license, which was granted eighteen months after it had been first revoked.

During the eighteen months that I was without my Large Goods Vehicle license I had sought alternative employment but no company would employ me. To them I was a compensation claim waiting to happen and so they would not touch me with a barge pole. That I suppose is a sign of the times in these litigious days.

Upon receipt of my LGV I once again approached BRS Taskforce who took me on and I was sent, once again, to work for EXEL Logistics, Trafford Park, on the Rover/BMW contract, delivering and collecting motor factors from various manufacturers. It was a pleasure to become reacquainted with all the ex- railwaymen that worked there, to be a part of their working practises and to enjoy the easygoing camaraderie that always abounds in railway and ex-railway depots.

I was not always sent on the Rover/BMW contract. If need be I would be sent to the Brighthouse contract working out of the old BRS Parceline depot on Barton Dock Road in Trafford Park.

Brighthouse was the new name and a re-branding of Crazy George's. Crazy George's was a group of furniture shops and warehouses that sold furniture to those on low incomes. The payments, for whatever household commodity was bought by the people that could not afford cash, were on a weekly basis and stretched over a long period, resulting in massive interest payments on the goods purchased.

The drivers that were sent by BRS Taskforce to work on the Brighthouse contract delivered bulk loads to the warehouses. Deliveries to Brighthouse customers were carried out by Brighthouse's own in house delivery service The Brighthouse warehouses were located at Warrington for the North West of England, Washington for the North East of England, Erdington for the Midlands, Bow for the South East and London, Uddingston for Scotland and another depot somewhere in the South East, to which I was never sent.

The Brighthouse warehouse deliveries were hard work with a lot of handball. There would be three piece, leather suites stacked three high at the bulk head which, after being lowered, had to be manhandled down the trailers forty four feet. Strangely enough the loaders at the Trafford Park depot loaded all the handball stuff to the front of the trailer and all the palletised stuff to the rear. Not a very good strategy for someone like myself, with a bad back.

The trip to the Scottish warehouse at Uddingston was, in the eyes of the management, a day run and true, it could be done in a day but only if everything went right. I, for various reasons had to take a night out, on a few occasions, on this run, usually ending up at the Truck Haven Truckstop near Carnforth. The same applied to the Bow warehouse. As far as the management was concerned the run to Bow and back was also a day run.

On both the Scottish and London runs I always took my overnight gear and quite frequently I was caught out; could not get back to Manchester and stopped at whichever truck parking facility I was nearest to when my driving hours were up.

Because of my back injury I was usually a bit slower unloading than the younger and more fit drivers and so I spent more nights out on these particular runs.

The pain I suffered on the Brighthouse contract led me to ask if I could be considered for another contract. The prince's Foods contract needed a driver and I was put on that contract. That meant six empty trailers a day from Trafford Park to Prince's factory in Miles Platting and returning to Trafford Park with loaded trailers over a twelve hour day. Each trailer was loaded from Prince's with twenty four tons of long life fruit juice, for distribution around the country.

That contract did not suit me because I no longer needed to work twelve hour days, besides the distance travelled between loading and picking up another empty trailer made the job a boring, tedious and monotonous undertaking. So I, once again asked for a move. This time I was sent to BRS trailer Hire on Nash Road in Trafford \Park. It turned out to be a job that suited me down to the ground. There was one other driver on that contract, A guy called George, who showed me the ropes. The job entailed delivery and collection of empty trailers from various depots around the country. There were a few nights out entailed but the job was a doddle because it was all driving and picking up and dropping trailers, there was a lot of running solo but there was no actual work entailed. Sadly after a couple of months on the job, BRS sold the concern to one of the big trailer rental companies.

BRS Taskforce was very accommodating and they put me back on the Rover /BMW contract. It wasn't long until things went wrong and I, unfortunately, suffered an industrial accident whereby I fell off a trailer and broke my ankle. That accident happened at a factory, belonging to Stadium Plastics, in Hartlepool which was the manufacturer of various components for Rover/ BMW/Mini vehicles. Not knowing at the time how serious the accident was I drove home from Hartlepool to the Trafford Park depot with a broken ankle believing it to be just a sprain. I was asked, by the EXEL foreman, at Trafford Park, why I was limping.

I explained about the tumble from the trailer at Hartlepool and was then asked to fill in EXEL's accident book, which I did.

My ankle by that time had become swollen and more painful but I decided, in my wisdom, that I was fit enough to drive my car home. That I did and when I got out of my car at home I found that I had difficulty in walking. I had to use the wall outside my house for support whilst I hopped on one leg to the front door. Upon entering the house and struggling to the living room I sat in my favourite chair and undid the lace of the boot on my right foot. My wife assisted in the removal of the boot and as it came off, pulling my sock with it, she gasped at the sight of the swollen, multi- coloured ankle. She suggested that I go immediately to the local hospital but I pooh-poohed the idea saying that I would go next morning.

The following morning, after a fitful night, I rose to find that I could put no weight on the foot and could not perambulate at all. The bruising on my ankle which had by then spread down to my toes and up to the calf of my leg had darkened to an almost black hue surrounded by purple, graduating in lightness to a mottled yellow. The swelling which, by then, was the shape of a small rugby ball was tight to the touch around the ankle getting spongier towards its extremes.

My wife took me to the local hospital where, after an X-ray, a fracture was confirmed. The leg was set in a plaster cast and it was thus encased for two and a half months. Upon the cast being removed it was found that my ankle bone had set and healed but my foot was at an odd angle and was facing in-wards which caused me to limp badly and drag my foot. It had an effect on my already suspect back and I was in great pain most of the time.

The hospital decided to fit me with a splint to attempt to pull the foot back to its normal position. I could not drive whilst wearing the splint, which I was told to wear for eight hours a day. I could only wear the splint, which I called my false leg, about the house; I could not wear it if I went out. The reason for that was that it squeaked so loudly when I walked around that it sounded as if I needed a shot of WD40 or a squirt of oil. My own GP decided that I was no longer fit for work and once again I was medically retired and put out to grass.

During the time I was on the sick and before I was medically retired, BRS; Taskforce had been bought out by another employment agency called the Blue Arrow Driver Agency. I was, therefore, no longer employed by an agency that held any connections to the railway's or its allied companies. It was the end of an era.

Lynx Logistics was recently taken over by UPS; the world's largest parcel and package Distribution Company.

EXEL Logistics was taken over by DHL; which originally stood for Dalsey, Hillblom and Lynn. DHL was bought out, in 2002, by Deutsche Post who also acquired Securicor Omega.

Pickford's became part of SIRVA Conveyancing UK in 2002; the largest moving, storage and relocation company in the world.

British Rail no longer exists due to the fragmentation and privatisation of all the rail companies.

Other railways' allied companies, such as Freightliner, have been through management buy outs; others have been swallowed up by their parent companies and no longer exist as part of the railways.

Thereby and sadly, ends my tales of the railways years.

Lightning Source UK Ltd.
Milton Keynes UK
175684UK00001B/34/P